How To Become
A Home-Based Wedding
Consultant And Make
Money

Additional copies of this book may be purchased directly from the publisher. To order, please enclose $49.95 plus $4 postage and handling. Send to:

Book Distribution Center
Post Office Box 51488
Ontario, CA 91761

Printed in the United States of America

0 9 8 7 6 5 4 3 2 1

TABLE OF CONTENTS

This page is intentionally left blank

FORWARD

HOW TO START A HOME BASED WEDDING CONSULTANT BUSINESSES

Many people dream of becoming their own boss and throwing off the shackles that come with working for someone else. You are one of them, searching for just the right business to start on your own.

Several things, however, may hinder you from taking that first leap out of the dungeon. Fear is probably the number one reason you hesitate. Striking out on your own creates fear in many forms. There is the fear that you might fail, the fear of the unknown and the fear of losing the security of a steady paycheck.

Along with these fears there are also several concerns and worries. "Do I have the discipline to be successful as my own boss?" "Do I have what it takes to run my own business?" "What does it take to run a business?" "Where can I find what I need to know?" Hundreds of questions run through your head when you think about starting your own business.

This self-study course is designed to help address those concerns and give you the knowledge you need to confidently start your own business and help you break out of those shackles. With careful planning, you can escape the dungeon of working for someone else and join the ranks of independent business owners.

One of the ways to break free from captivity is to become a wedding consultant. This is a home-based business you can start with a relatively low capital investment. Large wedding ceremonies have had a rebirth in recent years and the escalating cost of these weddings has swept the country, even in the smallest communities.

In our fast-paced society most people simply do not have the time to manage all the details of a complex social event like a wedding, yet they still desire to create the once-in-lifetime event of their dreams. But this desire comes with a price tag, and that creates a business opportunity that is waiting for you.

Over 2.7 million people will get married around the country this year, but few will use the services of a wedding consultant. Most never even think of turning to a professional consultant, but instead count on the florist, clergy or well-meaning friend to help them. Unfortunately the end result is often endless hassles and a wedding day that is so stress-filled there is little joy in the day. What should be an event to enjoy and remember becomes a nightmare of confusion and doubts because of their lack of experience with such a complex social event.

This is where you come in. After you complete this course, you will be able to turn even a very basic wedding into a significant source of income while you save your client both time and money in the process. You will be able to show your clients real savings and earn a nice living for yourself.

The service you have to offer clients is not affected by the economy, because even during tough economic times, a wedding is considered a one-time event that deserves the best.

Being a wedding consultant is something you can do no matter what your educational background or business experience. All you need is a little common sense, an ability to manage details and the ability to communicate with others. Everything else you need to know about running the home-based business of wedding consulting is covered in this course.

There is an estimated $27.4 million spent annually on weddings and the related services associated with the wedding. As a wedding consultant you can charge 15% for services you find for your clients as a fee, which means you could reach a six-figure income fairly easily. When you handle your clients with enthusiasm and professionalism, you set yourself up for success. The rewards are financial prosperity and the personal satisfaction you'll gain by being self-employed and helping young couples have the once-in-a-lifetime event they dream of!

Of all the many businesses you can start on your own, only a few let you start with a minimal investment. Franchises usually require that you invest rather large sums of money to carry their name and products. You are also limited by the business standards created by the original owners when they started their business. You must use and sell their products and in most cases follow their business plans. Most non-franchise businesses also require some kind of capital to get started i.e. capital to purchase products or supplies, to rent, buy or lease working space and other such expenses.

In addition to the investment of capital, all businesses require a substantial investment of your time and a resolve to learn all you can about starting the business, home-based or otherwise. You must also learn everything you can about the particular business you want to venture into. The more you learn about that business, the better prepared you will be to succeed.

In this course we'll help you get the knowledge you need to succeed. The course is broken down into two parts. Part one deals with establishing the home-based business of wedding consulting. In part two you will learn about all the specialized services that are part of making a wedding successful. In addition, you will learn how you can earn income from every aspect of the business.

The first part of the course gives you all the information you need to set up a home-based business as a wedding consultant. The last section of this course focuses on the cottage industries that surround the wedding event. All the services associated with a wedding from bachelor bashes to decorations provide unique financial opportunities for you. This guide covers most of the questions you have and provides you with much of the information you need to successfully run a full service wedding consulting business.

When you finish with this course you will have acquired the knowledge you need to start your own home-based wedding consulting business. Most, if not all of your questions will be answered and many of your fears and worries will be alleviated. You can strike out on your own, start your own home-based business and become independent. Few people get rich working for someone else, but the list of rich and famous is filled with people who started their own business and made it.

Although we cannot promise wealth and fame, this course can show you how to conduct a home-based business that can put you on the path toward success. Follow it and see for yourself.

NOTES

INTRODUCTION

IS THE HOME-BASED WEDDING CONSULTANT BUSINESS FOR YOU?

Who says you can't live a life of fairy tales? What is more fairy tale-based than a wedding? This book will prove to you that fairy tales are real and have been since the beginning of time. Few events match the excitement and positive anticipation of a wedding. The promise of eternal love and the hope of shared success fill the air as vows are made and gifts exchanged in a blended atmosphere of spiritual commitment and emotional excitement.

This fairy-tale like event is repeated hundreds of times a day across the country. Unless you are in the wedding business, that perfect day is usually a once in a lifetime experience, although some people experience that fairy tale event a second, and maybe even a third time. What could be better than making that special time happen for hundreds of people a year, without a hitch, while you make money, lots of money?

Most people have attended at least one wedding. Maybe it was a simple family affair or maybe it was an extravaganza of epic proportion. Either way, someone, somewhere, played a major part in putting that wedding together. Someone orchestrated thousands of details to make that special day a reality. The number of people who must be contacted can total in the hundreds and the cost of services provided will total in the thousands. Even a small wedding can cost between $2500 and $5000.

Why Is Wedding Consulting Such A Good Home-Based Business Opportunity?

The vast majority of people move from engagement to wedding, clueless of where to turn for advice, much less secure the services they really want in their wedding.

As a result they can become victims of high-priced services they do not want. Worse still, they receive inadequate services on the most important day of their lives, their wedding day.

In days gone by, families went to the local priest or clergy, who planned a basic wedding ceremony. But that day is gone. Orchestrating a wedding is as complex as conducting a major convention. Invitations, gift registry, reception hall reservations and music selection are just a few of the services that must be planned. Add to that gowns, flowers, cakes, photos, and meals and you have a massive task awaiting an un-expecting bride and groom, or those closest to them.

This lack of good information and the promise of a hassle-free wedding are reason enough to hire a wedding consultant.

For many, the wedding is a series a hassles and arguments that culminate in a major sigh of relief when the wedding is over, which is hardly a fairy tale ending.

If you adore the pageantry, glamour, beauty, solemnity, and detail of an exquisitely carried out wedding, then you are fully capable of helping others build these dreams for themselves. The home-based business of wedding consulting is waiting for your creative touch and experience.

This self-study course will take you through the steps required for creating a beautiful, sensitive, completely organized wedding. But, it's going to do much more than that. It will also take you through each of these steps and provide examples of how you can turn them into a successful and lucrative source of income as a wedding consultant. Whether you want to orchestrate the entire wedding or build a network of smaller home-based businesses, there is nearly unlimited financial opportunity.

By the time you finish reading this book, you will surely see a business opportunity that interests you. When you do, just pay attention to this information because in it, you will find everything you need to know about how to turn this opportunity into your own home-based wedding business.

The development of home-based businesses has grown considerably within the past few years. More and more people are deciding that working from home fits their lifestyle and financial needs better than working for other people. The downsizing of many corporations is another reason why many people are choosing to work from home.

As a home-based wedding consultant, it is up to you to decide how much time you want to spend working. You will also directly control how much you pay yourself. Your own time is the most important asset you will manage. Your overall income will be directly determined by how much time you decide to devote to the business.

One of the great advantages about this business opportunity is that you can make it a part time job, or a full-time job. The choice is yours.

How much money you make on each wedding is determined by the size of the wedding and the services you wish to supply. Wedding consultant fees range from $200 to $2000 a wedding, depending on the size of the wedding and the scope of the services you provide. One hundred weddings in a year and you are making some serious money, doing something you like, while helping couples and their families have the day of their life. What could be better?

In addition to consulting fees, many wedding consultants have specialty services they bill separately (for example, decorations, cake decorating, or gown design). These services can easily add up to an additional $50,000 a year. As a wedding consultant, you are positioned to offer your specialized skills in a most unique way.

Do you have what it takes to be a wedding consultant?

When you are the owner of your own wedding consulting business, you control the level of commitment you make to each wedding. Running a business, especially one that is run from your home, takes a lot of thought, discipline and planning. You will have to develop knowledge of the business in order to make professional business decisions. The beauty and idealism that your customers feel about their wedding will blind them to the business aspects of creating the wedding they desire. Mistakes or lack of attention to details on your part will not only be embarrassing to a bride and groom, but you can also lose a lot of money.

This book is about helping you make smart business decisions and avoiding the mistakes.

A home-based wedding consultant business requires personal stamina, organizational abilities, and extreme dedication, especially in the beginning. In some cases it also requires some start-up funds. You will not need an attractive office or a great deal of working capital if you are the primary service provider and you conduct your consulting services in the home of your clients. A majority of wedding consultants are women, but many men and even couples are starting their own wedding consulting business. But, whether male or female, married or single, anyone with fortitude and ambition can become a wedding consultant.

One of the most common reasons for failure of new small businesses like these is that the would-be entrepreneur goes into it with eyes not quite open far enough. It is imperative to do your homework first. Use the assessment on the next page to help determine your suitability for the home-based business of wedding consulting.

RATE YOURSELF AS A WEDDING CONSULTANT

Directions: Is wedding consulting a good business for you? Rate yourself on the following questions. Give yourself a 1 if the question does not describe you well, and a 6 if it describes you very well.

1. I am considered outgoing and friendly.

Low   High

1   2   3   4   5   6

2. I am comfortable meeting people and am considered a good listener.

1   2   3   4   5   6

3. I have a good eye for detail and am very effective at organizing and planning projects.

1   2   3   4   5   6

4. I am considered a self starter. It takes little external motivation to get me going on a project.

1   2   3   4   5   6

5. When given a project, I am able to stay focused until the overall goal is met.

1   2   3   4   5   6

6. I have a natural talent for handling multiple tasks and sorting out priorities.

1   2   3   4   5   6

7. I am considered an effective problem-solver and can handle disagreement positively.

1   2   3   4   5   6

8. I am comfortable bargaining and estimating prices, and when necessary can negotiate effectively.

1   2   3   4   5   6

TOTAL_____

Scoring: Total your results. Although no one can effectively predict business success, your results can be used as a starting indicator.

32 - 48   You seem to have many of the basic skills necessary to succeed in the home-based business of wedding consulting.

20 - 32   You have scored in the average area. There are enough questions that you scored low on to warn you about proceeding ahead to quickly. Take some time and review the questions above, and determine what you can do to either increase your score or find a way to accommodate areas of weakness.

Below 20 Before you read further, rethink the answers and review your talents. You have enough low scores to indicate caution. This is certainly no proof you will fail in the wedding consulting business, but it should be used as a caution.

Where Do I Start?

Reading and research are extremely important steps to take before beginning this or any business. Talking with others who have succeeded in a wedding consultant business will also be a great benefit. Nothing is better than the experience of others. Learn from their mistakes, rather than making them for yourself.

But will a wedding consultant really tell you what they know? Absolutely! The wedding consulting business is not a cutthroat business like many other businesses you could develop, which makes it an inviting opportunity. The wedding consultant builds business by providing positive, friendly and helpful information. As a group, wedding consultants are positive people to be around, and will most likely give you some time. People in general like to talk about their experiences and the wedding consultant is no exception. If you are open and honest about your intentions with them, most wedding consultants will meet with you over a cup of coffee or share a lunch with you. As your business grows, you may be able to share wedding projects with them or partner on occasions, so it's to the consultant's advantage to help you.

When considering weddings and how you can turn them into your own home-based business, many decisions must be considered. Anyone who has been to a wedding knows that a multitude of factors go into planning and carrying out a successful, beautiful wedding, one the bride and groom will remember for their lifetimes. Realizing your own financial dreams through the dreams of others makes this an even more exciting and fulfilling venture for your home-based business. It's exciting. Let's get going!

NOTES

_____

_____

_____

_____

_____

_____

_____

CHAPTER ONE

SETTING YOURSELF UP
IN BUSINESS

Sorting Fact And Fiction About Home Businesses

If you have friends or have met someone at a social gathering who works out of their home, you have undoubtedly either said to them or thought to yourself, "How lucky to be able to work at home." Many, if not all, of these work-at-homers probably smile and nod their heads in agreement. They know the advantages far outweigh the disadvantages.

Many of these home-based businesses provide information and services that today's busy people desperately need. Statistics show that over 32 million people are either employed in their homes or are employed by a company that allows them to work out of their homes. Predictions indicate that by the turn of the century at least half of all Americans will be working at home. More and more companies are finding that when they use the services of home-based businesses, they not only get highly skilled professionals, but also people who get the job done no matter what it takes. If these professionals have to work night and day to produce the results requested, they will.

If you're taking this self-study course, you are likely considering a change. You probably have at least one of five major reasons why people want to strike out on their own.

The first reason why you may be considering a change is that you work for a company and you would prefer not to. Your reason for this could be one of any number of things. You could be fed up with taking orders or you are tired of dealing with office politics. Maybe you think you can do better on your own, or maybe you just don't do well as a subordinate.

The second reason could be that you've heard rumors that your company is going to institute early retirement and downsizing. What once seemed a nice, safe, secure paycheck and job aren't so secure anymore. You face the very real possibility of unemployment. The thought of unemployment is more frightening than the thought of running your own business.

The third reason could be that you are already unemployed. You could be one of those already downsized out of your job. Or, you could be one of those in between jobs because you couldn't quite adjust to being a subordinate or to the office politics. You might be classified by the business world as "middle-aged," and you know your prospects are slim in this youth-oriented society and marketplace. Whatever your reason for being one of the unemployed, starting your own business can sound better than facing the unemployment office and sending out endless streams of rÈsumÈs each week.

The fourth reason could be that you want to start a family (or you already have started a family). You want the flexibility to be around while your children are growing up. You may still be working for a company and desire to quit, or you may have already quit in order to fulfill you vision of being a good parent. In either case you have decided your family comes first and that your career plans must adapt. The idea of working at home and near your growing children is foremost in your mind.

The fifth reason is that you see a chance to build a new business in an area that is not yet tapped. The days of the big wedding have returned. Most people do not understand how a wedding actually comes together, and since it is a once-in-a-lifetime event, they do not have the time to perfect their knowledge. As a wedding consultant, you can show them savings that more than pay for your services.

No matter what your reason for wanting to start a home-based business, it's an option worth pursuing. But before you begin, you need to look at what you are getting into, ask yourself a few questions and consider what is involved.

Considerations

As a wedding consultant, you can make a very good living. If you are willing to devote the time and effort, an income in excess of $100,000 a year is possible. Before you begin, however, one of the first things you must take into consideration is whether you have what it takes to run a home-based business. While you may not like taking orders from your boss, it is sometimes easier than giving orders to yourself, or dealing one-on-one with a disgruntled client. Being self-employed and running your own business takes a great deal of self-discipline.

One pitfall you may encounter are the attitudes of your friends and family. Although they love you and truly want you to succeed, it's hard for them to understand that even though you are working out of your home, you are indeed working. The wedding consultant works odd hours. And during the months of June,

July and August, you can easily be tied up 60 hours per week. You will work many long nights because that is when your clients are available, and then still have a full day of work scheduled contacting vendors. Many times your hours may be longer than your spouse's. Well-meaning friends and family will call or drop by whenever the urge hits them, unless you let them know firmly but gently that you do have a job to do. You will have to let them know what hours you have available for socializing.

Most successful wedding consultants share some common traits like family background, early experiences, motivation, personality characteristics, behaviors, values and beliefs. A list of these traits has been provided below. Read through it and see how you compare with these entrepreneurs. Evaluate your strengths and weaknesses as a potential entrepreneur by measuring how well these characteristics describe you.

Entrepreneurs:

- Were not outstanding students in school.

- Preferred individual school sports and activities.

- Started childhood enterprises like lemonade stands and lawn mowing services.

- Were daring kids who loved a good adventure.

- Were also stubborn children and rarely swung by the opinions of others.

- Are optimistic.

- Are easily bored.

- Are willing to work as long as it takes and even willing to go without sleep to finish a job.

- After successfully completing a project, move immediately to another.

- Are not deterred by failure-they often start a number of businesses before really succeeding.

- Are willing to commit their own savings and borrow from others to initially finance their business.

- Keep written goals for the long-term and short-term.

- Are able to deal with cash flow difficulties they encounter early in the life cycle of their business.

This comparison won't predict the success you'll have running your own business. It will, however, show you if you have an advantage or a handicap. The more similarities you see between these entrepreneurs and yourself, the more prepared you currently are for success.

Now that you see how you stack up against other entrepreneurs, look at whether you have an entrepreneurial personality. The following statements are designed to evaluate your personality traits. If most of these are true of you, then your personality is very similar to that of many successful entrepreneurs.

- I'm good at problem solving.

- I'm enthusiastic when I'm working.

- I enjoy a challenge and don't mind working hard to meet it.

- I can be very flexible when taking on a challenging project.

- I know how to do a job well and get it done quickly.

- I set goals for the future and work diligently to achieve them.

- I can express an idea in a unique way.

- I feel that results are not strictly left to chance, I have some control over them.

- I can make and stick to "gut-level" decisions.

- I can make firm decisions without regret.

You should now have a better idea of what it takes to be a successful entrepreneur. If you fall into a category that closely matches that of other proven entrepreneurs, starting and succeeding at your own business will be easier for you. That's not to say everything will fall in your lap, and you'll have instant success. It won't, and you won't. Whether you are a natural entrepreneur or not, running your own business involves a lot of very hard work and common sense, as well as learning all you can about running and managing a business.

The statistics say that the odds are against home-based or new businesses. They show an alarmingly high incidence of failure. Four out of five new businesses close their doors within the first three years of business. This is a failure rate of approximately 80%. Three of the main reasons new businesses fail are:

- Inadequate funding/financing;

- Poor management practices; and

- Ineffective marketing techniques.

Although these statistics sound daunting and you probably wonder, "Why even bother in the face of such odds," there are many businesses that do make it and provide a healthy income for their owners. There are techniques you can learn to put you ahead of the game. This book and course is designed to increase your odds for success.

Before we go further, let's look at some of the pros and cons of running your own business.

Advantages and Disadvantages

There are several pros and cons to starting and maintaining a wedding consulting business, just as there are with almost anything you do in life. To prepare you for life in a home-based business you need to be aware of these pros and cons. Knowledge helps you to combat any obstacles that come your way.

Let's begin with the advantages.

- You're there for your family when they need you. You get to watch your children grow up and be there to pick them up when they fall.

- You're not accountable to anyone but yourself for your time or whereabouts. You set your own workload volume and priorities. This could be both an advantage or disadvantage depending on how you handle it.

- Your clothing costs are reduced. You only need a few good suits or outfits for each season to wear when you meet face-to-face with clients. The rest of the time you can wear whatever you're comfortable in.

- You determine your own income. You can decide to make $20,000 a year or $100,000 a year. Your work schedule and priorities help you determine how much you make.

- If you prefer to minimize your activity outside your home you can. With wedding consulting you can handle a lot of your business over the telephone.

- If you're in a bad mood, you don't have to talk to anyone until your mood improves. You only have to show your good side to your clients.

- When you find yourself awake in the wee hours of the morning, you can use that time to work, earning a few dollars while your family is sleeping. When you can't sleep, use these peaceful, uninterrupted hours to be productive.

- You decide what you do each day rather than depending on a boss to decide for you. You are the master of your own fate.

- You get certain tax advantages because you use part of your home for your business.

- Checking the mail can be a pleasure now. Rather than just bills there are checks there for the work you've done.

- You set your own hours and decide how much work you take. No one dictates your hours or the amount of work but you. It's your discretion how much time you want to spend on your business and how much money you want to make.

- It can be fun.

Now lets look at the disadvantages of running a home-based business.

- You have to generate every dollar you earn by locating and selling clients who need your services.

- Many times it can be a long time between the checks you receive in the mail for your services.

- None of your benefits such as insurance, health, life, disability, pensions, vacations or sick leave are furnished for you. You have to arrange and pay for all these yourself.

- Although there are some tax advantages to a home-based business, there are also tax disadvantages. These are discussed later in this book.

- Your office is so close to you that unfinished business and deadlines can seep over into your allotted time with your family or your personal time.

- When office equipment fails, you have to pay outside help to repair it rather than rely on in-house, company-paid personnel to handle it for you.

- Nothing gets done unless you do it. You can't delegate responsibilities to others until you grow to the point where you can afford to hire a staff. Therefore it's up to you to keep supplies on hand, to do all the work and to handle all the problems and emergencies that crop up.

- Your time is your money. You don't earn a penny unless you physically do the work, all the work. You no longer get paid vacations, sick leave and such. If you don't work, you don't get paid.

- You are totally alone in this venture. There's no one but the four walls of your office to bounce ideas off of.

- Until you train them otherwise, friends and family don't realize that you are working. Although you're home all the time, they will drop in at the worst times æ like when you're on a deadline.

- At the beginning and often long afterwards, work and revenue both can be a cycle of feast and famine.

These advantages and disadvantages give you an idea of what you face when you start a wedding consulting business. Study them carefully, they give you clues as to what you need to plan for. You will need to make contingency plans to overcome the disadvantages.

Now that you know some of the pros and cons of running your own business and your strengths or weaknesses as an entrepreneur, you next need to evaluate yourself and your skills.

Evaluating Yourself

All businesses must communicate in order to survive. Because you depend on relationships with both vendors and clients for your livelihood, you must be a good communicator. You must also be able to assess client needs and develop solutions to their problems. So not only do you need to be an excellent communicator, you must also be a good problem solver and negotiator.

When you were trying to find employment working for a company, you had to evaluate your skills in order to prepare a rÈsumÈ and to present yourself in a favorable way to those who were making the selection decisions. Take the time now to evaluate yourself so that you can consider whether creating a home-based business fits your skills and qualifications. The skills inventory form on the next page will help you with this evaluation.

Skills Inventory

Directions: Start with your most recent position and list your job titles, dates and any skills you used or learned while in that position. You may also include any volunteer activities or civic duties in which you have participated.

Job Title	From	To	Skills
_____	____ / ____	____ / ____	_____
			_____
_____	____ / ____	____ / ____	_____
			_____
_____	____ / ____	____ / ____	_____
			_____
_____	____ / ____	____ / ____	_____
			_____
_____	____ / ____	____ / ____	_____

Look at your list very carefully. With a highlighter or pencil, mark the skills you like the most, the ones that made you happy, or that you looked forward to doing. These will help you to find the discipline to work alone in your home-based business. Compare your list of skills against the list of skills needed to succeed in your home-based business. If you see a gap there, decide what you need to do to improve your skill-base. This might involve learning new skills or boning up on the ones you already have. You might have to take courses, however, this isn't your only means of honing skills. You can also join professional organizations, read, take part-time jobs in your industry and attend seminars relevant to the subject you want to learn.

Determine what you need to do to bring your skills up-to-date. Then design an action plan for yourself. In this action plan set up two columns. In one column list what you need to do and in the second column give yourself a deadline to meet your action plan goals.

Another solution to help you get your home-based business off the ground and acquire the skills you need to succeed is to get yourself a mentor. A mentor is someone you can turn to for advice and assistance when you need it. Choose someone who is currently working as a wedding consultant. If you can't find someone in that field, find someone in a similar field. This person must be successful and someone you can respect and trust.

This person will be a valuable resource for advice and recommendations, and they will be an important source of emotional support. They have already mastered many of the obstacles and hurdles you will face and know what you are going through. They can lend a sympathetic ear when you need one. Do be careful, though, not to abuse this relationship. Mentors can help you get through the rough times and supply you with invaluable information; however, if you try to take advantage of them, they will not hesitate to withdraw their aid.

Goals

Before you take this giant step into your future, you need to take a close look at your life and what you want to do with it, then ask how a new business will affect it. You should not venture into the wedding consulting business, or any other business without a plan. The plan becomes your road map to keep you steered on the right course. While you are planning for your business success, you also need to plan for your family success.

You are going to need extra time to dedicate to this business venture. Is your family ready for this level of commitment? You may be strapped for cash. Do you have adequate reserves to sustain yourself as you get started? You may find yourself frustrated and discouraged; do you have adequate support to sustain your efforts? You may need professional assistance; do you have at least one mentor who can help you?

It is important to remember that this is a real business. Do not treat it as either a hobby or a toy. Both attitudes are a guaranteed "fast track" to embarrassment and bankruptcy.

Personal Goals

One thing you'll want to consider is your style of living whether you are willing to give up certain luxuries, at least in the short term, if necessary. Talk to your family about the changes this venture will have on them and your lifestyle. Until you get established, you and your family are likely to have to make sacrifices.

While many of your job-related expenses are reduced when you decide to work out of your home, so is your income, for awhile at least. Many of the expenses that were paid by the company you worked for will become your personal responsibility. For instance you now have to furnish your own business insurance as well as your equipment and supplies. All of these things must be considered as you plan to start your own business.

While planning for your business you should begin with your personal goals, both your own and those of your other family members. These goals may include income, education, investment, vacation and retirement goals. Whenever you set goals, it's important to write them down. Keeping them only in memory is not as effective as having a written record to which you can refer. Our minds tend to change things as we go along. The act of writing them down, will also make them more specific, which in turn, will increase the likelihood of your achieving them.

Your personal goals should describe what you want to achieve for you and your family. As you plan your personal goals, be as specific as you can be. Don't worry about whether you will be able to meet a specific goal. If a goal reflects a driving desire you have, it will be sufficient to motivate you, and you'll achieve it.

Define your goals in terms that will help you achieve them. Be specific about what each goal is. For instance, if you are defining an annual income goal, state in terms of actual dollars.

At the same time be careful not to set goals that are impossible to attain.

Once you have your goals laid out, set up a way to track and measure your progress toward meeting them by breaking your list into pieces. Every segment should have a deadline and an outcome that is measurable.

It is suggested that you set up two personal goal plans. One should be your goals for the next year and the second should be for the next five years. Review your goals from time to time and evaluate your progress toward meeting them. Remember these goals exist to motivate you and are the reason you will struggle through the tough business days and long hours.

As you are planning your personal goals and before you plan your business goals, assess your personal financial situation. This lets you see where you are now and lets you plan on how to improve so that you can meet your goals.

Needing money and being hungry for more work and income are excellent motivators. However, when you have more expenses than income, the stress that places on you and your family will negatively impact business.

By planning for your financial needs, you can be more selective about the work that comes your way rather than taking anything that comes along. Clients sense when they can take advantage of your lack of capital. When you work from a sense of security, you are better able to take work at fees you set rather than fees the client sets. Fees that clients set may not always be the best fees for the work you have to perform. Respected professionals rarely haggle over fees.

Experts advise that before you begin your venture into self-employment, you have enough money set aside to cover your business start-up costs, overhead and living expenses for a minimum of six months, but this is only a recommendation. Many businesses have started with far less and yet manage to succeed. It's not impossible, but it does make it a lot easier when you have a safety net.

As you assess your own financial situation, you need to decide the risks you're willing to take, and determine what, if any, sacrifices you are willing to make. Get familiar with your personal expenses (if you aren't already) as well as how much money your family needs to survive each month.

Next figure out how much income you can rely on from other sources: spouse's pay, investments, severance pay, savings, etc. At the same time you're examining your expenses and income, determine what expenses you can cut. Most people starting up a new business find it better to start lean and then relax the budget rather than see things getting tighter and tighter. Cut as many unnecessary expenses as possible. You will need to get by on this cut-back budget until your business grows to the point this special budget is no longer a necessity.

When you are setting up your personal budget make it a part of your personal goals. Include in your business goals the steps that will allow you to increase your income so you can afford more luxuries for you and your family. Work toward earning enough from your business so that you can ease the strain a tight budget puts on you.

Part of your goals should be to plan for and build toward the time when you can pay yourself and give yourself a bonus from the budget. A sure sign of success will be when you have outgrown this "special budget."

If you think you need to borrow money, borrow it while you are still employed. Most lending institutions won't consider a loan application from someone who's self-employed until they have two years of self-employed income tax returns they can show as proof of income.

Set up a personal budget for you and your family. Use the following worksheet guideline to create your own.

Personal Budget Worksheet

Item	Amount per Month	Item	Amount per Month
Savings and Investments (paid out)	_____	School Related Expenses	_____
Shelter	_____	Gifts	_____
Mortgage or Rent	_____	Debts	
Home or Renter's Insurance	_____	Credit Cards	
Taxes	_____	Other Debts	_____
Utilities	_____	Entertainment / Leisure	
Maintenance and Repairs	_____	Dining Out	_____
Transportation	_____	Movies/Theater	_____
Car Payments	_____	Travel	_____
Auto Insurance	_____	Club Dues and Fees	_____
License & Registration	_____	Recreational Dues and Fees	_____
Property Taxes	_____	Books, Magazines, Newspapers	_____
Fuel	_____	Hobbies	_____
Parking fees	_____	**Other Expenses**	_____
Maintenance	_____	**Total Monthly Expenses**	_____
Other Transportation costs	_____	**Income Sources**	_____
Necessities	_____	Spouse's Income	_____
Groceries	_____	Investment Income	_____
Insurance	_____	Unemployment / Severance Pay Income	_____
Personal Care	_____	Other Income	_____
Child Care	_____	**Total Monthly Income**	_____
Clothing	_____	**Total Monthly Income Needed**	_____
Tuition and Fees	_____		
Housekeeper	_____		

As you are writing your personal goals and plans, make sure they are related to your business. In other words, tie your personal goals into your business goals. Then use your personal goals to verify your business goals. The two go hand-in-hand, and when used together help you succeed in your business venture.

Business Goals

As you begin formulating your business goals, follow the same steps you used for your personal goals, but focus those steps on the outcomes you want for your business. Set up written one-year and five-year goals for your business just as you did for your personal goals. Keep these in a safe place where you can review them from time to time.

As you're planning your business goals, you'll want to consider the following factors:

- anticipated profit, short term and long term;
- business growth expectation;
- services to offer at the beginning and later; and
- the need for hiring staff to assist you as you grow.

After you have your business goals compiled, begin thinking about how you will achieve them by creating a business plan. This business plan acts like a road map to keep you on course as you venture into your home-based business. The busier you get, the more you'll rely on your map. You also may need to use your business plan to secure financing at some point.

Creating a business plan is a simple way for you to organize your thinking. You might consider it in your action steps. In your planning you determine the time and resources you need to reach your goals.

A business plan helps you work things out on paper first and lets you set up systems to handle everyday needs. It provides a map for your business operations, and gives you a place to gather your bearings when business problems arise. A business plan, when done properly, frees you up to handle the things that matter most and lets the business run itself. It also allows you to have the time and energy to handle any road blocks or unexpected occurrences that crop up from time to time.

If you plan to borrow money for your business start-up costs or to finance any part of your business, you will need to have a business plan ready. Lending institutions want to see a business plan that demonstrates your abilities, business structure and projected sources of future revenue. This business plan is what you use to sell these lending institutions on taking a chance on you and your business.

Business plans are broken into five main sections. These sections are as follows:

- **Executive Summary:** The Executive Summary is the first part of a business plan lending officers read, it's the last part of the plan you write. This section sums up your business, your business approach and your qualifications. The Executive Summary gives the lender reason to read the rest of your plan. In this section you should summarize the business. This includes the name of your business, its address, the business structure, target market and your main business activities. Be very concrete and specific in your descriptions. You might also include some competitive information. Also included in the Executive Summary is a clear reason the business exists and why it will be profitable.

- **RÈsumÈs of Owner(s):** This second section of your plan describes who you are (and others if you have partners) in rÈsumÈ format. Here you should highlight career achievements that support your business and plan. Keep this section down to one or two pages at the most. Use a reverse chronological order to list the positions you've held. List accomplishments and results for each position that you will use in the business you are planning. If you have examples of your work you can include, attach these as a special appendix to the plan. Use this same format and include rÈsumÈs of any partners you have. If you plan to have partners or staff, it is a good idea to explain their expertise in relationship to the business. This is the section where you need to sell your personal worth. A good test of this section should be a "yes" answer to their question, "If I sent this information to a client, could they buy my services?"

- **Business Structure or Form of Organization:** In this section describe the type of structure of your business. If you are operating as a sole proprietorship, a simple paragraph stating this fact is all you need. If you have partners, you need to include all the partners' names, titles and a description of the roles they will be playing in your business. Also, list the authority or responsibility they have in the business. If you are asking for a loan, financial backers want to know if other parties are sharing the risk and will assume responsibility for paying back any obligations the business assumes. As you prepare this section of the business plan, you will get the first indication of any potential future problems with relationships and partners. If you can't clearly, easily and comfortably write this section, think carefully about who you want to have in your business. If your business is a corporation, state that fact and list the names and titles of officers and directors as well as their ownership interest. Also include a copy of your Articles of Incorporation and Bylaws in a separate appendix. To enhance your standing in the lender's eyes, include a list of Professional Advisers including professionals and organizations you've used to help you develop your business. This will show lenders you are serious about your business.

- **Financial Statements:** This section may include your personal assets depending on the structure under which you choose to operate. You can, of course, let your accountant   compile these for you to add credibility or at least let your accountant review them   before you use them. Along with your Personal Financial Statement, you should also include a Personal Income Statement, Business Start-up Expenses, Business Cash Flow Projections and Total Start-up Capital being sought. Each of these are covered in more detail later in this section.

- **Marketing Plan:** This section describes the services and/or products you are going to market. You need to show market potential here and how you plan to reach your clients and sell your services or product.

Although a marketing plan can take many forms, you should include:

- The product and services you offer;

- Pricing and a comparison of your pricing to existing products or services;

- Promotional strategies which should include an explanation of how you plan to advertise your services, how much you expect to spend on these promotions and a fairly detailed explanation of how many promotions you will run over the course of a year;

- Demographic information about your target market, describing who they are, why   they would buy your product or service, and a projection of how big this group is; and

- Competitor information, including the availability of their services. A good business knows who the competition is and why they can compete against it.

Following are samples of a Marketing Plan, Personal Financial Statement, Business Cash Flow Projections and an example of the information you should include in the Start-up Capital Needs section. To begin with, let's look at a sample Marketing Plan. In this Marketing plan, include specific promotions, schedules and costs.

Marketing Plan

Name of Business:

Name of Owner:

Owner's background, experience and accomplishments:

Description of services and products:

Pricing and comparison of existing products and services:

Target clients and industries:

Demographic information:

Differential advantage: (how you add value to your customer's organization)

Marketing and promotion plans:

Hourly rate and project fees:

Competitive information:

The Personal Financial Statement should include all your assets and liabilities. The following worksheet can be used as a guideline and converted to our business plan.

Personal Financial Statement

Assets   Value

Real Estate (include appraised value)

1. _____ $_____

2. _____ $_____

Automobiles and other vehicles

1. _____ $_____

2. _____ $_____

Savings and Checking Account Balances (list account numbers)

1. _____ $_____

2. _____ $_____

Stocks, Bonds, and Other Securities (list each holding and number of shares)

1. _____ $_____

2. _____ $_____

401(k) and other such personal investment pensions

1. _____ $_____

2. _____ $_____

Antiques, Art, Jewelry, Furs, Collections

1. _____ $_____

2. _____ $_____

Other Personal Property (household furnishings, etc.)

1. _____ $_____

2. _____ $_____

3. _____ $_____

Other Assets (specify)

1. _____ $_____

2. _____ $_____

Total Assets $_____

Liabilities   **Balanced Owed**

Mortgages

1. _____ $_____

2. _____ $_____

Home Equity Lines of Credit

1. _____ $_____

2. _____ $_____

Charge Cards

1. _____ $_____

2. _____ $_____

Auto and Other Installment Loans

1. _____ $_____

2. _____ $_____

Promissory Notes Made to Others

1. _____ $_____

2. _____ $_____

Margin Account Balances with Brokerage Firms

1. _____ $_____

2. _____ $_____

Other Liabilities (specify)

1. _____ $_____

2. _____ $_____

Total Liabilities $_____

Net Worth (total assets less total liabilities) $_____

For the Business Cash Flow Projections you should include a six-month or one-year spreadsheet showing income figures increasing each month. Be sure to build this information as realistically as possible. Financial backers know that businesses don't boom overnight, so you won't be able to fool them. The best gauge of whether your cash flow projections are accurate is to answer the question, "If this were my minimum, could I live and continue to grow?"

The following worksheet will help you to start projecting your business cash flow. Some of the areas in this worksheet may not apply to your business. Use the ones that work for you and discard the rest.

Business Cash Flow Projections	
Projected Monthly Income	$_____
Cost of Goods Sold	$_____
(types of goods or services)	$_____
(types of goods or services)	$_____
Total Cost of Goods Sold	$_____
Gross Profit	$_____
(projected monthly income less total cost of goods sold)	
Expenses	
Office Supplies	$_____
Telephone	$_____
Postage/Shipping	$_____
Publications	$_____
On-line Services	$_____
Bank Fees	$_____
Utilities	$_____
Debt Service	$_____
Promotional Costs	$_____
Temporary Services	$_____
Cleaning	$_____
Maintenance	$_____
Travel	$_____
Entertainment	$_____
Professional Dues	$_____
Accounting and other Professional Services	$_____
Business Insurance	$_____
Others (list)	
_____	$_____
_____	$_____
Total Expenses	$_____
Net Profit/Income (gross profit less total expenses)	$_____

In order to determine the total start-up capital you will need, here are the expenses you should total:

✔ **personal expenses for six months,**

✔ **equipment and supply costs,**

✔ **marketing and promotion costs, and**

✔ **overhead expenses for six months.**

The following example gives you a guideline for how to include this information in your business plan:

Start-up Capital Needs	
Monthly Personal Expenses for Six Months	$_____
Start-up Costs for Equipment and Supplies	$_____
Start-up Costs for Marketing and Promotion	$_____
Projected Monthly Business Overhead Expenses for Six Months	$_____
Total Needed	$_____

We suggest you identify both one-year and five-year business goals for your new business. You can then use both goals along with your business plan to help you measure how you are doing, so that you can easily identify course corrections you need to make along the way. These goals and your business plan will also be valuable tools to help you secure financing if you need it. You should plan to review your business plan every month.

What You Need

After you have created your goals and business plans, it's time to start thinking about the specific needs of your business. These include equipment, supplies, space, and time. These are important considerations you must plan for. Let's take a look at them one-by-one.

Equipment and Supplies

Since you are venturing into a home-based business, your expenses for equipment and supplies are much less than a company that has many employees. You will generally meet your clients in their offices or their homes, so you don't have to have extravagant furnishings. Comfortable and functional will work very well when you are starting out.

More than one successful business began at the kitchen table, but if you plan to claim the tax advantage of a home business, you need to set aside both space and equipment dedicated exclusively to your business. The basic equipment you need will probably include a desk, a comfortable desk chair, a file cabinet and bookshelves. You can find many of these at a reasonable cost at second-hand shops or garage sales, if you don't already have these furnishings. Since you are starting out on a tight budget, economy is the keyword here. Remember fancy isn't a priority, functionality is.

Next you need to consider your communication equipment needs. This includes your phone, fax and modem for your computer. Although you can get by with one phone line, you really do need at least two phone lines to run an effective home office. The two basic lines you need are one for your business line and one dedicated to your fax/computer modem. If you prefer and can budget it in, you can also have a third line for your personal/family use. This is, of course, the ideal situation; however, you can work around this if you have to with only two lines into your home. Your business line can function as your personal line until you can afford the third line. A dedicated line for your fax/computer modem is almost an essential because clients and suppliers need to be able to send a fax without having to call you first to make sure that you know there is an incoming fax on the way.

Many newer computers have a fax/modem already installed as part of the package. If your computer doesn't have one installed, you can purchase one at a reasonable cost (under $100) at a computer or office supply store. You should be aware, however, that these internal fax/modem cards only allow you to send faxes that are generated from a program within your computer. You can receive faxes from anyone, anywhere with no problems. But if you have a document in "hard copy" that you did not generate on your computer, you won't easily be able to fax it. Your choices in this case are to use a scanner (an additional, questionable expense at this point), or take the document to a "quick print" store and ask them to fax it. Many mail-stop stores have this service available. This may be the best option for you if you don't have a great need to send faxes. The other option, if you can fit it in your budget, is to have a separate fax machine. The cost of these machines has gone down drastically in the past ten years. Shop around your local computer or office supply stores for the best price.

There's one more option if you don't already own a printer. For less than $1,000, it's possible to purchase a laser printer that is also a fax machine. As you consider these choices, minimizing your start-up costs is your number one priority, so making the occasional trip to the quick print store, may be the first choice.

For your telephone service needs, many telephone companies offer services that can help you run your business more effectively. Check with them to find out what they offer and their fees. Some of these include answering service or voice mail services that take messages for you when you are gone or on a call. Of course, there also are the options of call waiting, call forwarding, conference calling and other services the telephone companies offer. Decide which of these services are the ones you need and budget them in.

Another near necessity for your business is a computer and its peripherals. Peripherals include your software, extras and your printer. There is no right or wrong type of computer to own, but the best advice is to select a system you're most comfortable with. The same goes for your printer æ go with what you can afford. While laser printers are best, you can get by with an inkjet at a fraction of the cost of a laser printer. Your are printing your public image every time you print, so select wisely. Even an invoice, when printed on your machine should look professional.

The first decision when purchasing a computer is whether you will buy an Apple/MacIntosh system or a PC Microsoft Windows-based system. If you have no experience with either one, check out both. Look into the price differences and ease of setup and operation, and then pick the one that you are more comfortable with. If you already have more experience with one than the other, you're better off buying that system so that your learning curve will not be as steep as switching systems.

As you are comparing computers you need to consider certain, basic, must-have features. Here are some of the basics you need with your computer system. The most important feature to your computer is its memory and disk storage space. The minimum memory you should consider for a computer these days is 16 megabytes of memory, especially if you plan to use Microsoft Windows 95 as your operating system. For hard disk space you need a minimum of 1 gigabyte and more would be better. Today's memory and storage prices are at an all-time low, so you can buy quite a lot of memory and hard disk for modest prices.

The CPU, Central Processing Unit, is the brain of your computer. This unit should be at least a 486 running at 66 MHz (megahertz), if you are buying a used computer. If you purchase a new PC computer, you will not be able to find much less than the equivalent of an Intel Pentium 133 MHz processor. The faster the processor, the faster you will be able to perform functions on your computer.

A CD-ROM drive is not essential to your computer. Most new computers, however, will have them already installed. Most of the software available today will be packaged on CD-ROMs. It could be to your advantage to have this feature as part of your system. It certainly speeds up software installation time when you install from a CD-ROM rather than from diskettes.

As mentioned earlier, a modem is essential to your business. Generally the modem in your computer functions in a dual role. It functions as your fax machine and can also function as your modem to connect to the Internet or other online services. Some of the newer computers have pre-installed programs that also let your computer function as a telephone complete with answering machine and speaker phone. The minimum modem speed you need for your machine is a 14,400 bps. A new computer with a modem installed will have a modem with a speed of at least 28,800 bps, and many will be 33,600 bps. Once again, gaining more speed is primarily a matter of cost.

When you are selecting a computer to purchase, keep in mind the expandability of the system you want to buy. As you grow, your computer needs will grow also. Purchasing a computer that has the capability for being upgraded will save you the cost of purchasing a whole new system a year or two down the road. It's much more cost effective to install a larger hard drive and more memory than it is to purchase a whole new system.

What software do you need for your computer? Several of the programs you'll need come pre-installed on most of the newer systems. Most PCs come with Microsoft Windows 95 as the operating system. Microsoft Windows NT is another operating system choice, as is Windows 3.11 on the PC-type of computer. Most home-business computer users will find Microsoft Windows 95 the easiest all around choice if they purchase a PC. If you purchase an Apple/MacIntosh computer, the operating system choice is already made for you.

You also need a word processor such as Microsoft Word or Corel WordPerfect as part of your normal business operations. Both of these programs will handle your mailing needs such as mail-list management and mail-merge. **For your account management and accounting you need the following programs or types of programs:**

- a contact program such as Act!, or Outlook.

- a program for accounting and bookkeeping like Quicken, QuickBooks or M.Y.O.B.

- a spreadsheet like Lotus 1-2-3 or Microsoft Excel.

An optional piece of equipment you might need is a copy machine. If you plan to do a lot of copying, then purchasing this piece of equipment is ideal for you and your business. If your copying needs aren't that great, however, it's more cost effective to use a near-by copy center or mail store rather than investing precious capital in this machine. You may also need to consider whether to obtain postal equipment. If you do, two machines will take care of most of your mailing needs: a postage meter and weight scale. Both are available to you through vendors such Pitney Bowes or Avcorp. For other resources contact the U.S. Postal Service.

One additional question to answer as you consider your equipment needs: should you lease some or all of the equipment? Leasing gives you the option of retaining more of your start-up capital. It also may give you some tax advantages. You can use a depreciation schedule to determine deductible expense for purchased equipment. The actual expense of leased equipment may be fully deductible. It's important to involve your CPA or another qualified tax expert as you consider the impact the purchase-or-lease decision will have on your business taxes.

The last thing on your list of needs for your office is office supplies. Following is a list of most of the essential supplies you need for your office:

- copy or printer paper (white)
- fax paper (if you opt for a fax machine)
- Rolodex and extra cards
- file folders and labels
- hanging files, tabs and indexes
- stapler, staples and staple remover
- tape and tape dispenser
- lined pads
- Post-it(R) notes
- paper clips
- envelopes
- computer disks and disk holders
- pens and pencils
- highlighters
- pencil sharpener
- desk light
- scissors
- printer ink or cartridges
- copier ink or cartridges (if you opt for a copier)

Shop around computer and office supply stores as well as discount stores in your area to find the best prices for the things you need. Don't overlook the option of purchasing some of the equipment you need from thrift stores, second-hand stores or even from garage sales. You can also consider shopping around at some of the discount warehouses like Sam's Warehouse Club. Sometimes you can find brand names at these warehouse stores for much less than you would have to pay at a department or specialty store. Remember economy is important when starting out in your home-based business. You can always upgrade later when your business grows and allows you to.

Space

As you are starting out, you want to start small and at the least expense possible. Therefore, plan to run your business from your home until you have adequate cash flow to move into leased office space. Some very successful wedding consultants never move out of the home office.

Because you will be meeting clients at their homes, there is really no need for the extra expense of a separate office. Most of your initial contacts will be via the telephone and mail.

Your working area or space is the next most important consideration for your home-based business. This space is where you are going to be spending all of your working hours; therefore this area should be comfortable, adequate and well-lighted. Where you designate that space is up to you and the allowances of your home. The ideal space for your home office is a spare room with outside access and the ability to block yourself off from the activities of the rest of your home. Most people starting out, however, may not have this luxury. So the next best option is a spare room in your home with a door you can close to block out distractions. Be sure to let the rest of your family know you are working and are not to be disturbed. Select a room that allows you enough space to put your desk, file cabinet, bookshelves and other office equipment.

For those working with very limited space, it may be necessary to make do with a corner of one room in the home. If this is your situation, set up a space in your living room, dining room or even your bedroom for a desk with phone access, room for your printer and a small bookshelf. If this is not an option, then you can improvise and use your dining room table as your desk during working hours and for its intended use during personal hours. Of course these are temporary solutions for the usage until you can either create a larger area to work with more privacy, or rent a small office outside your home.

As your business grows, you may want to consider the option of renting space outside your home. Chapter Five covers leasing office space in more detail.

Time

While you are considering all options for your home-based business, you also need to consider your time. Think about how much time you have to devote to your business and how much time you want to devote to the business. Take a look at your business goals and plans and review them carefully.

If you want to pursue this home-based business as a part-time investment of your time, you can certainly do that. Many parents choose this option until their children begin school and therefore free up more of their time.

If you have more ambitious goals and want this home-based business to be your new career, then you will want to devote more time to it. Examine your business and personal goals closely and determine how many hours you are willing to put into your business. You can decide to put in only the typical eight-hour work day or as many hours as it takes to get the results you want. One of the great advantages about the wedding consulting business, is that you can invest as much or as little time as you want and as they fit with your personal and business goals. Since this is your business, the hours you devote, especially at the beginning, are directly proportional to the amount of business and income you will generate. Remember, if you don't work, you don't get paid. Everything about this business is totally dependent upon you and the effort you put into it. The decision of how many hours you work is up to you and you alone.

CHAPTER TWO

WHAT IS A WEDDING CONSULTANT?

The Definition of a Wedding Consultant

A simple definition of a wedding consultant is that he or she helps prospective brides, grooms, and their families plan their ideal wedding. A wedding consultant can also be referred to as bridal consultant, wedding broker, wedding coordinator or wedding planner. The wedding consultant helps a bride and groom with every step and detail of planning and coordinating their wedding. The wedding consultant helps them with budgeting for the style and scope of the wedding they want. Next the wedding consultant helps with detailed planning of things such as location, food, wedding cake and reception refreshments, invitations, flowers, photography, videos, transportation, entertainment and more. Then the wedding consultant confirms and follows up on all these details for the bride and groom. And finally the wedding consultant makes sure all the details are in place on the day of the wedding, and then handles any glitches that may occur during the day.

The goal of the wedding consultant is to offer the bride and her family peace of mind by managing every aspect of their wedding while staying within an agreed budget. The wedding consultant stays on top of the planning and orchestrates each service as it occurs, making it possible for a bride and her family to enjoy the occasion, hassle free. In the final analysis, the success of a well-planned wedding is the complete responsibility of the wedding consultant.

A good philosophy adopted by many wedding consultants is that the bride and groom are deserving of anything they want and can afford. They are the ones in charge, and as such are allowed to create their own "rules and regulations." The wedding consultant provides information and details so the clients can determine for themselves if they wish to follow conventional wedding practices or diverge and establish their own unique wedding event.

Characteristics of A Wedding Consultant

Not all people have the necessary personal attitude to perform as a wedding consultant. Some of the characteristics that are needed in this job are a pleasant, helpful attitude, motivation and initiative, ability to work with emotionally stressed people, organizational skills, empathy, good judgment, good business sense, responsibility, dependability, assertiveness, flexibility, dedication, creativity, and tact.

Wedding consultants also need to like people. Poise, tact, and flexibility will help them work well with all kinds of people. They must have confidence, optimism, and enthusiasm. They must also have a sense of style.

Consultants must work well under pressure. They must have the temperament to enjoy the occasion and at the same time keep the wedding organized and on track. They must also respect and be knowledgeable of the religious beliefs and customs of different faiths and ethnic groups.

Consultants should be creative and artistic. A flair for the dramatic is an asset. At the same time, they need common sense to manage both time and money. An outgoing personality and a sense of humor will stand them in good stead at all times.

Good rapport, communication, and a feeling that the couple can rely on their consultant is vital to the teamwork. A good consultant will go the extra mile and resolve any disputes between the bride and family members. The consultant acts as the couple's liaison, smoothing over rough spots that sometimes come up during the period leading up to and on the wedding day.

Although a new wedding consultant may not have all these attributes, it would be beneficial for them to acquire as many as possible in order to have a successful business. Perhaps, most important is to know yourself. Know your strengths and weaknesses. If you do, then you have a good chance of developing the attitudes and skills you need to succeed.

Why Do People Select a Wedding Consultant?

Do you know of any couples who are planning a wedding? Are they slightly overwhelmed at the thought of planning an extravagant event, but are confident they can pull it off? Many couples, as they learn too late, are at a loss when it comes to coordinating such an event. If they possess little or no experience in planning complex events, a professional wedding consultant - you - is definitely in order.

One of the most valuable services rendered by a wedding consultant is relieving the wedding party of the details that can take them away from fully enjoying the special occasion. The wedding consultant lifts the burden of planning and execution from the couple and their parents.

The decision to hire a consultant is based on several factors. For many, they don't have enough time. Full time jobs do not allow the phone calls and visits required. Major oversights often occur when people have limited time. The ability to stay organized and focused often seems impossible.

If the bride is new to the area and has few friends or family members close by, planning a wedding without outside help could become a nightmare. A bride planning an out-of-town wedding can be overwhelmed with the task of making wise choices, especially with today's high-priced wedding services.

Whatever the reason, the wisest choice is to hire a professional.

Couples spend thousands of dollars on their wedding and they want things done well. A wedding consultant will ensure that the wedding day will be one of fond memories, not "bloopers" and embarrassments. Almost one-third of couples who handled their own weddings said that they wished they had used a consultant. The concern and worry about whether everything would come together, robbed them from fully enjoying a very special time.

A wedding consultant has the time that the bride and groom do not. The consultant will refer the couple to wedding service providers who have solid reputations for quality and value for the price of the service. The consultant will orchestrate the event with its many service providers and vendors so that the wedding day runs smoothly. With the assistance of a wedding consultant, the couple can make the most of their wedding budget and avoid costly mistakes.

Consultants can save money by setting a realistic budget and prioritizing the desires of the client, so that the money is spent on what's really important to the couple. The wedding consultant will help find the best wedding service providers at prices the couple can afford.

Wedding consultants will also help the couple find the balance of tradition and individuality that will suit their personalities and desires. They will help design the wedding in a way that follows tradition to the extent the couple prefers while reflecting their personal tastes, whether the consultants plan formal or informal weddings, large or small. They help couples and their families with all or some of the details of this event. Observing traditions and etiquette and taking care of the practical tasks of a wedding require expert advice and guidance.

Wedding consultants help brides and their parents create an appropriate budget for the costs of the wedding and then help them keep within that budget. They may also explain the traditions of the weddings to the parents of the bride and bridegroom in terms of who typically pays for what.

They also assist with the monthly planning schedules, wedding day schedule, and reception floor plans. The following wedding checklist can be a valuable resource when working with clients.

MoneyMaker Tip: This checklist can be effectively used when meeting new clients. By using this checklist, the wedding consultant can clarify how much time the client is willing to spend in the planning of the wedding and what can become contracted services.

THE WEDDING PLANNING CHECKLIST

Six to Twelve Months Before the Wedding ...

Wedding logistics

[ ] Meet with clergy: _____

[ ] Wedding Date: _____

[ ] Time: _____

[ ]   Site: _____

Build your wedding budget

Identify attendants, ushers, ring bearers etc.

Groom	Bride
_____	_____
_____	_____
_____	_____
_____	_____
_____	_____
_____	_____

Resource comparisons

[ ] Compare facilities for rehearsal and reception sites

[ ] Compare caterers

[ ] Bakers

[ ] Florists

[ ] Musicians

[ ] Photographers

[ ] Rental party services for chairs, tents, glassware, etc.

Wedding Garment Selection

[ ] Select bridal gown and attendants' clothing.

[ ] Select clothing for groom and his attendants.

[ ] Mother's clothing choices to coordinate with wedding.

Stationery

[ ] Decide on invitations

[ ] Announcements

[ ] Thank-you notes.

[ ] Draw up final invitation and announcement lists

Miscellaneous

[ ] Create wedding gift registry

[ ] Meet insurance agent to insure rings, wedding gifts, etc.

[ ] Decide on honeymoon location reservations.

Two to Three Months Before the Wedding ...

Certificates

[ ] Get birth certificates

[ ] Physicals

[ ] Blood tests

[ ] Wedding license

Activities

[ ] Address and stamp envelopes.

[ ] Decide music for wedding and reception

[ ] Meet photographer

[ ] Take black/white newspaper photo.

[ ] Confirm flower orders, rose petals, confetti, etc.

[ ] Complete arrangements for rehearsal dinner

[ ] Complete arrangements for reception

[ ] Verify menus with caterer.

[ ] Order wedding cake and groom's cake, if desired

[ ] Check on bridesmaids' gowns and shoes.

[ ] Obtain measurements for ushers and order clothing.

[ ] Choose gifts for all attendants.

One Month Before the Wedding ...

Fittings, Sittings & Clothing

[ ] Break-in shoes

[ ] Check final fittings on bride's and groom's clothing

[ ] Sit for wedding portrait

[ ] Write announcement for newspaper

[ ] Pre-wedding showers and parties

Arrangements

[ ] Arrange transportation and lodging for wedding party

[ ] Select gifts for bridesmaids and groomsmen

[ ] Confirm hotel accommodations and honeymoon tickets

[ ] Schedule hair appointments.

[ ] Determine place for bride to dress

[ ] Determine place for groom to dress

[ ] Determine places for attendants to dress

[ ] Pick up marriage license

[ ] Assign someone to handle and deliver gifts after reception

Begin setting up new living quarters

[ ] Arrange utilities

[ ] Phone

[ ] Mail

Stationery

[ ] Mail invitations

[ ] Write thank-you notes for gifts opened before wedding

One Week Before the Wedding ...

Confirmations
[ ] Photographer
[ ] Florist
[ ] Musician
[ ] Baker
[ ] Verify number of wedding guests
[ ] Inform caterer of final number

Final Preparations
[ ] Perform final alterations on attendants' clothing
[ ] Pack for honeymoon trip
[ ] Write or prepare place cards for reception and dinners
[ ] Spend at least one quiet evening with respective families

The Day Before the Wedding ...

[ ] Lay out wedding clothes
[ ] Pack bride's and groom's going-away clothing
[ ] Pack toiletries
[ ] Make out check to clergyman or other officiate and the musicians.
[ ] Attend rehearsal dinner.

The Day of the Wedding ...

[ ] Be sure to eat a good breakfast.
[ ] Get dressed for the wedding.
[ ] Thank everyone for attending and helping.

After the Wedding ...

[ ] Mail wedding announcements, if you use them
[ ] Write remainder of thank-you notes
[ ] Invite family and wedding party as your dinner guests

[ ] Live, love, laugh and be happy!

How a Wedding Consultant Conducts Business

A wedding consultant works mostly by appointment. You may spend five hours meeting with a bride and provide services totaling 40 hours. The total time depends on what you are hired to do. For example, you may be asked to handle only some of the services needed for the wedding, such as only the reception. Or you may be asked to be involved in the selection and purchase of the bridal gown. In another instance you may be asked to coordinate all the events of the wedding day itself, a process that takes significantly more hours. Each client's needs are different.

Wedding consultants do much of their work by phone, and they must have a car or vehicle that can transport and deliver a wide array of wedding supplies. Wedding consultants must also spend a great deal of their time working outside their office. They may be asked to shop with clients or for them, check decorations, and look at sites of weddings and receptions. Many couples marry in parks, hotels, and homes, as well as in churches. The consultant must constantly review each potential wedding site to ensure facilities meet client expectations.

The wedding and all its different aspects need to happen perfectly, and the wedding consultant must do everything in their power to make that happen. In order to ensure things happen the way they should, the consultant has many responsibilities. These include consulting on the style of the event, assisting the wedding party with pre-nuptial events such as bridal showers and bachelor parties and making certain that all vendors involved arrive on time and prepared. In general, the wedding consultant will troubleshoot for anyone who lacks the time or know-how to put on the event correctly and efficiently.

On a typical day, the wedding consultant spends most of their time scheduling appointments over the telephone, networking with vendors and meeting with the bridal couples. For example, your first meeting of the day might be with a bride, discussing different reception plans, such as deciding whether to choose among buffets, cocktails, sit-down dinners, and hors d'oeuvres for the reception.

Once the consultant sets up an appointment, the bride, usually with the groom and/or the mother of the bride meet, often in their home. Just in case the client insists on meeting somewhere else, you may schedule the appointment in your office. If this is not a good place to meet, you may pick some location such as a restaurant or the lobby of a nice hotel.

MoneyMaker Tip: Often new businesses find it difficult to afford an office that befits the quality of their wedding services. Many insurance offices, and small businesses are closed during the hours you meet with your clients, since most wedding consultants meet in the evening when their clients are off work. Low cost rent can usually be arranged. In fact, your own insurance agency may allow you to use their office space in an "on-demand" basis for very little cost.

The initial meetings are the critical ones. That's when everyone confers on the date, location, and budget of the wedding. Many of your clients may be upscale individuals who can budget between $13,000 and $20,000. Others may be as low as $4,000 to $6,000. The conversation generally turns to money within the first few minutes of your meeting, so you must be prepared to address the subject of your fees, and the range of services and prices that are available. The bride often comes prepared with at least an idea of how she wants the wedding to be developed, but may have little comprehension of the overall costs, or degree of detail that must be managed. After establishing the budget, they will typically discuss the style of the event, for example, whether it is to be formal or semi-formal or even simple.

No matter what the budget, it is imperative that each client receive your full attention to detail and wishes.

If the wedding is to be at a home, the consultant will know where to rent awnings, tents, tables and chairs, canopies, display tables, as well where to obtain aisle cloths and other miscellaneous items. The wedding consultant should also have lists of printers and engravers for printing wedding invitations, suppliers of glassware and china, caterers, and bakers who make wedding cakes. They also need lists of florists, musicians, photographers, and beauty salons whose hairstylists help brides and bridesmaids.

MoneyMaker Tip: It is always difficult for people to talk about money, especially when they may not know the wedding consultant very well. By having approximate costs for each service printed in a list, the client can very quickly assess the level of service they want and build a budget to match. They easily recognize that your are interested in helping them manage their costs.

Many times customers will know of stores that have bridal gift registries, but the well prepared consultant will have a more complete list of stores and their services as well as how effective the stores are in providing this service.

Additional services of a wedding consultant may include knowing the cleaners who have the ability to clean heirloom clothing. They will also be prepared to make arrangements with car rental agencies and limousine services.

Music and Entertainment

As for entertainment, the wedding planner should be prepared to highlight local bands, string quartets and disc jockeys. Experienced wedding consultants know that having several audition videos of bands can help secure a contract.

MoneyMaker Tip: This is one of the least expensive ways to build your credibility as a wedding consultant. Bands are eager to play at weddings, and they will provide you with audition tapes free. Just make the contacts and ask.

Sometimes the consultant will send the client to see an act in person, since there are many styles and formats of music. Make sure that you know what kinds of music the couple prefers; then match that with the musicians. It's also important to determine if the band can play requests if this is what the bride and groom prefer.

Never underestimate the importance of good music and its contribution to a wedding. The ability to match the music to the bridal couple's preferences is very important. It's also important to keep ethnic music preferences in mind. For example, one would not want to go to a Polish wedding and have classical music softly playing in the background, even though in their home, they may often appreciate classical music. Dancing the polka late into the evening hours is part of a cultural expectation for those attending a Polish wedding. Different nationalities of people often have preferences for special music and it is very important to be prepared for this.

Many times in ethnic weddings, the bride and groom already have their favorite band in mind and will be sure to tell you. An experienced wedding planner will be acquainted with bands that play at ethnic weddings as well as bands for weddings without an ethnic character.

MoneyMaker Tip: If you have some doubts about your ability to match musical preferences, you probably already know someone who is musically talented. Ask them for help. If you describe the kind of wedding and the people involved, they will be able to contribute significantly to your success. Before long, you will have the necessary information and will no longer need their input.

Food and Catering

Food and catering eat up the large part of the wedding budget. Together, the consultant and the clients decide on the complexity and extravagance of the food that will be served in connection with their wedding. Events involving food can include a rehearsal dinner following the wedding rehearsal (typically the night before the wedding itself); a wedding breakfast after a morning wedding; a wedding lunch; and a wedding reception. Some weddings may include both a wedding breakfast and a reception. For each of these events, the important decisions are the style of meal to be served as well as the menu.

Types of meals may include buffet, sit-down service, or family style. It's also possible, if the wedding is in the early afternoon, that the clients will choose to provide only cake and punch at the reception. Whatever the decision, the consultant should keep a file of menus from various caterers designed to fit within specific budgets. Some wedding consultants have found it advantageous to maintain individual files of menus for breakfast, lunch and dinners. In the presence of the bride and her mother, this is another way you can show your ability to organize even such small details as separate file for separate meals. Of course, the consultant can arrange for any specialty food not found on the menus, and retain that information future use. An experienced planner will be sure to find caterers who can serve ethnic types of food for Italian, Polish, Jewish, Mexican or other ethnic weddings.

Other Wedding Services

Once some of the big-ticket items are settled, the consultant concentrates on details like invitations. The planner displays a book of different typefaces and will have samples of finished invitations on hand. The wedding consultant also consults on the flowers and the cake, showing pictures or videos from her vendors. Much of the time, the planner should be prepared to make recommendations from among vendor's used in the past. This is one of the main areas where the consultant had better be confident of the vendor's abilities and reliability. The planner must know the standards and costs for each supplier. It's important to realize that your reputation will be affected by the quality of those supplying services for the weddings you plan. You have to be confident that your suppliers will deliver the service on time and as requested. Your client will judge you by all the things that happen at the wedding you planned, and they will tell their friends. Indeed their friends will be participants in the event, whether it's a success or a failure.

Planning and Paying for Cost of Services

The outcome of these early meetings is the development of a balance sheet that you prepare listing all the services, the cost for each service and the schedule for when the services must be paid.   Some clients build an escrow account that the consultant draws upon. Other consultants pay all bills and then forward the costs, plus a carrying charge to the client. In other cases, the customer pays the invoices as they come due, or they may elect to make all the checks out in advance and give them to the consultant to distribute.

Each vendor is likely to have their own policies about payment. Some may not perform the desired service until they have received the agreed upon amount. For example, limousine services are usually paid two weeks in advance. The band is typically paid the night of the event. At early meetings, the clients and consultant determine the most hassle-free way to manage all payments.

One issue that must be planned for is cancellations by some person or facility booked for the wedding. The wedding consultant should always have a backup, another reception hall, or another photographer for example. The longer you stay in business the more you will build relationships with vendors who will support and bail you out in tough situations. Always have a solution for every potential problem.

These planning stages can take some months, but the clients get an unlimited amount of the consultant's time for their money. As a rule, wedding consultants will have from three to six months to plan weddings. Now and then, however, they must plan an entire wedding in as little as two weeks. In busy seasons it is common for wedding consultants to work on several weddings at the same time.

Not everyone who calls the consultant wants the full wedding treatment. Many clients may prefer that the consultant just book the band or handle the floral needs, for instance.

Budgeting for Wedding Services and Controlling Costs

Evaluating the cost of weddings depends upon several factors. You must consider the couple's budget, the size of the wedding and what the bride wants: both her fantasy wedding and her reality wedding.

A wedding can be very expensive. It's important for you to be sure you understand what the couple really wants. Sometimes they will not be clear in their own minds about what they want. Your task will be to help them sort it all out so they have the wedding they can live with and feel good about. For many couples the most valuable service you will render is helping them strike the proper balance between the elaborateness of the wedding and the cost of the wedding.

Many people are uncomfortable with the word "budget," but it is the best way to avoid any misunderstandings between you as consultant and your client. Once you and the couple have reached an understanding about the type of wedding they want and the money they want to spend, it's time to create a written budget that will record in black and white what services, including yours, will cost. You should also state in this document the method of payment you expect for your services and for the services of all the vendors who will be involved. Putting all this in writing will avoid any misunderstandings later on when the bills start coming in and the wedding date draws closer.

One of the great advantages to the couple in having this written budget, is that it will reduce some of the uncertainty about what things are going to cost. There will be no hidden or unexpected financial surprises they will have to deal with later on.

As you begin to discuss the details of the budget and the services, it will soon become clear to the couple what an advantage it is to them to have retained your services. They will begin to see the discounts that you are able to attain that are not available to the general public, nor to them if they had not hired you as their wedding planner. You will have clout! Because you will handle hundreds of weddings and bring customers to service vendors, you will be able to negotiate special discounts the clients themselves could never obtain. You will also be able to obtain "perks" from time-to-time that further increase the value of the services you provide.

Your job will be to create a realistic budget and hire skilled people who fit within the defined budgetary constraints. There is no sense in spending unnecessary money when discount services may meet a customer's need. You will be able to plan ahead and prevent over-priced, panic buying. Clients will not have to pay for hidden costs on sites and services or for guests who don't show up.

Your knowledge will also enable you to get more for the client's money while staying within their budget. As an established consultant, you will have a wide selection of vendors and valuable connections. This will be of great assistance to the bride because you will know who to book and when, you'll be able to provide price comparisons, oversee vendor contracts, avoid overtime charges and save on services when guests don't show. All of this collectively will result in considerable savings to the couple. The couple benefits by getting the feeling of a more elaborate wedding.

Time goes so quickly on a wedding day. The wedding consultant can orchestrate the day and ensure the wedding is memorable and calm. All weddings have glitches, but a good consultant makes sure the client never has to deal with them or even know about them. By making sure things run smoothly and on time, the consultant saves the client incredible time and cost. For example, one hour of over-time at a location or with a photographer can cost between $400-600!

Additional Wedding Consulting Services

Wedding consultants help brides choose their wedding gown and supervise the fittings. They help plan the color scheme, may help mothers and bridesmaids choose gowns or dresses, and give bridegrooms, fathers, and male attendants advice on correct wear. They may also help brides select a dress or suit to wear when leaving the reception.

The consultant may give advice on the style, wording, printing or engraving, and mailing dates of invitations, thank-you notes, and other announcements. They may order invitations and announcements, address them from lists supplied by the bride, and mail them. The wedding consultant may be called in at any stage in the wedding plans, from beginning to end.

One of the initial obstacles a wedding consultant must overcome is the idea that they cost the client money. The truth is the consultant will save money while maximizing time and reducing stress. But putting a price tag on those benefits is not always easy. If a couple truly wants a beautiful day and a hassle free wedding, the consultant is actually a necessity, and just as important as a caterer or photographer.

The possibility of one-stop shopping, supplying everything needed for the wedding, from clothing to photography, from musicians to reception hall rental cannot be overvalued. People trust their car to a professional and they trust their investments to a professional; why wouldn't it be natural to trust your most special day to a professional?

The closer it gets to the wedding day, the role of wedding consultant switches from booking agent to one of detail manager. In a big wedding, there are hours of time invested to confirm all elements of the wedding will fall into place. The wedding consultant is on the telephone often, keeping the bride and groom apprised of who gets paid when.

MoneyMaker Tip: As the wedding day draws closer, it is important to make regular contact with your client. It is a good business policy to send a weekly report of your activities. This assures your client you are working for them and provides peace of mind. Keep these reports positive and upbeat. The client needs to know everything is OK. They do not need to know the negative aspects you are managing. These reports should build confidence that everything is going to go smoothly as a result of your efforts. This will pay off in referrals later on.

During the actual ceremony, the consultant moves on to the reception location. The consultant makes sure the flowers and food are in place and may even handle last-minute tasks like laying out table numbers and place cards. A big wedding is seldom flawless, but the consultant is prepared for almost any emergency so that it 'appears' flawless. The consultant stays through much of the reception, acting as a genial liaison with the couple and the caterers. The wedding consultant may also lend a hand if food service appears to be going too slowly, and can even be found providing extra napkins when necessary.

This extra pair of hands on the wedding day is priceless. The consultant will ensure that a schedule for the event is well planned, written and distributed to all the service providers involved in order to provide for a smooth-running event. Details such as coordinating and overseeing vendors, supervising and cueing the wedding party and music, and assisting with seating arrangements are just a few of the duties a consultant will assume. These are all things that the bridal party should not have to think about. A bride can rest assured knowing the wedding day will be handled with care while she relaxes and enjoys her glorious day.

It is important to keep yourself emotionally distant from the proceedings. Otherwise, your involvement in so many weddings will be adversely affected and can wear you down. When a guest tells you how nice the wedding is, not realizing that it was you who planned it, that's when you know you are in the right profession. And when the bride and groom tell you that you "made" their wedding, the satisfaction of hearing that will bring you the ultimate pleasure as a consultant. The best wedding consultants are invisible; only the most careful observers should ever know the role they play in the wedding.

CHAPTER THREE

HOW DO YOU BECOME A WEDDING CONSULTANT?

Why hire a wedding consultant?

Jeremiah and Sandy spend a wonderful evening canoeing on the lake in the moonlight. Jeremiah sings a song of love to Sandy as he cautiously kneels on one knee in the canoe, looking across at his chosen lady. He lifts a dark, velvet box from his pocket and opens it. Moonlight strikes the diamond, sending shimmering rays into Sandy's tear-filled eyes. He slides the glittering ring onto Sandy's waiting finger, asking that age-old question. As expected, Sandy responds positively, and they seal their engagement with a kiss.

The man and woman are ecstatic, overwhelmed and a little crazy, now that they've decided to get married. With so many things to plan, this is a busy time. They have never been involved in a wedding and do not even know where to start. All the questions about who to contact, what is acceptable protocol and how to make sure that nothing is left out begin to bubble to the surface, and soon their relationship is filled with stress and more than a little disagreement.

It's a long walk to the altar. Ask any bride or groom. Couples glow when they announce their wedding. But, that glow can turn to gloom, however, as they prepare for that wedding. Decisions await and haunt them: reception, photographer, flowers, food. Long before the bridal march down the aisle, this couple will spend months planning the ceremony, arranging the reception, and enduring more stress than most executives will in any major business. And since more and more brides work, the hassle of planning a wedding is further magnified.

The way for Jeremiah and Sandy to save time, money and avoid stress is for them to hire a wedding consultant or coordinator. For many, getting someone else to take over all these responsibilities is worth almost any amount of money, and that's good news for American bridal consultants. When the couple hire a wedding consultant, they still make decisions but relax while the consultant wrestles with details.

Couples in America now spend more than $27 billion a year on weddings, and the bridal consultant is earning more and more of that amount each year. Big, traditional weddings are staging a comeback and have brought with them the problems of organizing such a complex event. Busy couples are saving time and headaches by turning over these problems to the wedding planner.

Want to spend all your free weekends attending weddings without being a party crasher? Pursuing your dreams of becoming a wedding consultant may be a worthwhile endeavor.

How can I take advantage of changing wedding traditions?

In the "olden days," around the turn of the century, during the opulence of the Victorian age, wedding planners helped brides sort through the maze of social customs that surrounded a proper wedding. Today, a good bridal consultant can still offer advice on etiquette, but that's just the start of the wedding journey. One of the most important services a consultant can provide is access to the best vendors at better prices than if the couple had found the vendors by themselves. This gives couples a real advantage on finding the perfect site, the most lavish flowers, and the right caterer.

Traditions have a way of distorting over time, and what is considered acceptable today can be considered tomorrow's major social gaffe. In contrast to their Victorian counterparts, today's planners stress individuality, not set standards. This change in traditions opens the door to your new business, because many of basic questions young couples as have to do with wedding etiquette.

Make sure you read up on wedding etiquette. Even though many weddings nowadays don't follow the strict traditional etiquette, it's vital that you be learned in all aspects of proper wedding etiquette, rules and procedures. You can be much more creative when you knowingly violate traditional standards than when you do it out of ignorance. The greatest artists and composers became great because they were well grounded in the "rules" of the day, and then creatively broke them intelligently.

MoneyMaker Tip: Few people can make money on wedding etiquette, but it is one of the best ways you can build credibility with potential clients. Review the local wedding traditions in your community and build a page of common practices. You may want to include a section describing Victorian protocol to provoke conversation and interest. This list can be given away, handed out when first meeting a client or offered as part of a marketing campaign. Your knowledge in this area addresses your client's earliest questions and implies you probably have knowledge and expertise in other areas of the wedding.

Study and practice over time will help you master all aspect of the wedding. Wedding etiquette is a good place to begin. The skills necessary to oversee and plan weddings that go off without any wrong moves in not far away.

Although big weddings are back, they aren't necessarily following traditional wedding etiquette to the letter. Successful consultants work with clients to create unique events - even if that means fulfilling unusual requests.

What are the financial constraints of wedding consulting?

Let's take a look now at some of the financial issues involved in the wedding consulting business. The first issue is the uncomfortable, but necessary matter of discussing your fee with your clients.

How a wedding consultant approaches the sensitive area of money is critical to the wedding consultant's success. Often the first question a young couple will ask is, **"How much will it cost to have you help us with the wedding?"** You will know that because of the savings they will gain by using your services to get the kind of wedding they want and can afford, your services will actually cost them nothing. Unfortunately they won't be able to see this until after the event.

You can't really answer this question until they've answered some questions for you. A good way to deal with this question, especially if it's one of the first questions they ask, is to say something like, "My fee is based on the size of the wedding and on the services you decide to use at your wedding. So before I can answer your question, I need to have you answer some questions for me. Then I'll be able to tell you exactly what my services will cost."

It's important for you to communicate from the beginning that your job is to create a wedding they can be proud of and one that stays within their defined budget. The service of a consultant is analogous to fees a travel agent charges. The agent finds the best possible fare for their client, and they make a fee off that ticket. They may make more money from a higher fare, but they will not stay in business long.

Next it's important for you to make sure that your clients understand each of your services that are available, and their approximate cost. Your services may range from handling only one aspect of the wedding, such as the reception, to handling the entire scope of wedding services. Once you've developed a clear picture of the wedding the clients want and plan to afford, you can then intelligently consider your fee options for that particular wedding. A flat fee might be appropriate for one customer, while another may prefer a fee based on a percentage of the total cost of the wedding.

Budgeting is the major asset of the consultant's job. An effective consultant should be able to work within any budget and help clients get the most for their money. Setting the budget will be one of the first services you will provide to your client. This point, more than any other, is the basis for a successful wedding consultant business. If you please the bride and groom in this one area you will see your business grow by leaps and bounds.

MoneyMaker Tip: A preprinted list of every possible wedding service can be a big help in setting your fees as a consultant. The stark reality of wedding costs may mean some clients will cut back on their wedding while others will decide to do some things themselves. This list shows what can be done. By providing this list you reinforce your knowledge as a professional and equip your client with the best buying decisions and smart buyers make good customers!

Research, Research and Research Some More

You can start a wedding consultant business with less than $7,000, sometimes with no money at all other than beginning expenses. But, don't let the low investment fool you. This is not a get-rich-quick business.

One of your first moves in becoming a wedding consultant is to join the International Association of Bridal Consultants. Within this organization, you will learn more about the wedding consultant business than you ever thought possible, and you'll also have the opportunity for networking with other consultants. It's a wonderful way to learn the trade of consulting. They have an exceptional network of people you can network with and you can gather information on certification programs offered for bridal consultants. Here's their address:

International Association of Bridal Consultants

200 Chestnutland Rd.

New Milford, CT 06776-2521

(860) 355-0464

To be a good consultant, you must do your homework. The most important first step when you begin your business is to locate professional, reliable vendors. Visit all the local sites. Consult with every florist, photographer, stationer, videographer, disc jockey, and band in your area. Be sure to check references for every vendor you contact. The more thoroughly researched your list of vendors, the more valuable it is.

In addition to research, you'll need patience. Bridal consultants don't advertise through the usual media, although they can. Referral is the primary method of getting the word out. This kind of advertising is cheap, but it is not fast. As mentioned earlier, many experts recommend starting the business part-time while working at a regular job. In time, your business will grow into a full-time venture, but in the meantime, you can rely on an additional means of support.

Once you learn all there is to know about the business, you can then decide what parts you want to be involved in, and there are many. You may choose to specialize in one aspect of the business, such as focusing exclusively on reception arrangements or on clothing arrangements for the wedding. More likely you will want to develop an ability to consult on all the aspects of the wedding. This will mean more profit for you and greater savings for the bride and groom and their families. As you gain experience you'll learn where to cut costs without sacrificing any of the beauty or elegance of the wedding. You will learn how to work within a budget a little later in this book.

From Pleasures Come Profits

Most women still want elaborate weddings. And with so many women in the workforce, they can now afford them more than ever before, but they don't have the time to invest in planning them. That's where you come in. Most weddings these days will average between $6,000 and $20,000. The average wedding in the US costs $16,485. If the couple places high importance on having an elaborate, prestigious wedding and they have a large guest list, the cost can easily be higher than the average.

TODAY'S WEDDING STATISTICS

The Couple (first time marriage)

- Average age of bride is 24.5 years old

- Average age of groom is 26.5 years

- 2.3 million weddings take place a year

    Source: *Washington Post*

Costs

- Wedding related retail sales are estimated at $32 billion a year.

- The cost of the average wedding $16,485

- Sale of wedding gift related purchases is $7.8 billion a year

- The average engagement ring costs $2807

- The wedding dress costs $725

- Wedding limousine fees average $192

- The average wedding reception costs $5,957

    Source: *Bride's Magazine*

The majority of planners charge 15 percent for their services. This means this business can prove to be quite lucrative. Planning a $10,000 wedding will net you a $1,500 profit! And, considering that you can plan more than one wedding at a time (although you must give each wedding your individual and full attention) your profits are really unlimited. If you live in a larger, affluent community, your business profits could be dramatically higher.

Though prices and methods of billing vary, $2,500 is not unheard of for planning a major wedding. Some planners charge a percentage of the overall budget while other planners charge flat fees of $1,000 or more, depending on the number and type of services rendered. Additionally, you may also collect commissions from vendors. This way, you can charge your clients less and still bring in a tidy profit.

Established wedding consultants bring in annual net profits as high as $123,000, though the average full-time operation probably nets closer to $57,000. For many veteran wedding planners, the financial rewards aren't the only compensation. The creativity and excitement of planning the perfect wedding is also a source of fulfillment.

The number of weddings that a professional and knowledgeable consultant can handle per year can average around 40, with the consultant also assisting in part with as many as 150 additional weddings. If the average budget for those 40 weddings is only $10,000 (a relatively low number) and you charge 15 percent, each wedding would net you $1500. That $1500 multiplied times 40 weddings a year will generate for you $60,000 per year. And, if you assist with only portions of 150 additional weddings (such as organizing the bridal showers and bachelor's parties) netting approximately $200 per wedding, that is an additional net income of another $30,000. Combine these two, and the consultant is generating a gross annual income of $90,000. If you have done a good job of managing your expenses, this can be a very attractive income for doing something you truly enjoy while knowing that you brought pleasure and peace of mind for many brides and grooms and their families.

While a capital investment is needed to own a pre-existing bridal consulting business, there is no investment needed to become a bridal consultant. There are expenses, however. These include business cards and advertising in the Yellow Pages and in the bridal supplements printed by churches and newspapers. The first year, a wedding consultant should reasonably anticipate earnings of $18,000 to $25,000. Your level of motivation determines how high you go. It is reasonable to expect increases of eight to ten percent each following year.

Whatever you do, learning as much as you can about the business and its standards before launching full swing into the wedding consultant business is one of the first and most important steps you can take.

It's important for you recognize that the schedule of a consultant can be an exhausting one. With one-third of all marriages taking place during June, July and August, the peak wedding season, the consultant can expect to work 50 to 60 hours a week, which can include attending a wedding nearly every weekend. Because the work takes a consultant out of the office much of the time, it is very useful to employ an answering service to field calls. Your clients will want to be able to contact you to answer questions and discuss arrangements at any time. You need to be easily accessible to minimize the likelihood of their getting frustrated with their inability to get in touch with you. An answering service and a cellular phone will be valuable assets in creating confidence that you are devoting your full attention to their wedding.

To the client, their wedding is the only wedding taking place, and certainly the most important. While you may be managing as many as ten weddings at one time, they want to feel like theirs is the most important one you are handling.

You also need to be easily accessible to your vendors. Chances are at least one involved in each wedding you are handling will have some kind of crisis. You'll be better able to manage the crisis if they can easily contact you and you can easily make the calls you need to make as soon as possible.

When you are not working with a client, you will be busy working on getting new clients. Many referrals are through word-of-mouth. You can augment these with introductory letters sent to potential clients. Even though the number of people employing wedding consultants has dramatically increased in recent years, the concept of a wedding planner is still strange and unknown to the majority of potential clients. Therefore, it's a good idea to ask your vendors to recommend you by offering incentives to the potential client. Attending wedding trade shows is another important way of contacting and finding potential clients. Most of those attending will be there to obtain information for their wedding. At these shows, the consultant accepts clients on a first-come, first-served basis, eliminating the problem of having to handle two big weddings on the same day. Your local papers and the International Association of Bridal Consultants will be good resources for learning when wedding shows occur in your area.

Being your own boss pleases most people. The downside is that the large amount of time the wedding consultant puts into the business leaves the consultant with precious few private hours, especially during the peak wedding season. You will have to devote some of your leisure time to networking with and studying vendors so you can stay current on the wedding service vendors in your area. The more comprehensive a wedding's consultant's business network, the greater flexibility the consultant can offer clients.

As your the business grows, you may develop a staff of consultants who do much of the busywork of wedding planning like following up on vendors. This staff may be subcontractors, who work only on consignment, or full time staff. That would give you time to concentrate on administrative responsibilities and client meetings.

CHAPTER FOUR

THE WEDDING CONSULTANT'S ROLE

Taking the First steps in Wedding Consulting

Everyone starts their business from a different place. Many people find themselves pulled into the business of wedding consulting because of a friend's needs or because they discover after conducting a grown child's wedding that they enjoyed the process, even the hassles. Sometimes wedding consultants seemed to fall into the business because they provided one service for a wedding such as flowers or cake decorating, and through this discover that clients needed additional assistance. Whatever your initial motivation, here you sit reading a book and hoping you can make sense out of all the different aspects of wedding consulting.

Complexity, the very thing that makes wedding consulting so emotionally appealing is also the thing that makes it difficult to get started. If you examine most home-businesses, you will see that most offer only a small niche product line and probably never approach the complexity and fascination of wedding consulting in terms of the wide range of products and services that are offered.

This chapter is designed to help you get past the apparent obstacles presented by the complexity of services and products. We will clarify some aspects of the wedding that may be unclear, and we will provide you with a number of basic forms you will need to conduct your business as a professional. Although forms and paper are not an exciting part of business, they can make getting started a great deal easier. Feel free to copy these forms and use them with clients. You may want to have many of them professionally photocopied and distribute them as part of your initial marketing strategy.

Let's start with some fundamental issues you will face with your every client.

Choosing the Best Man and Maid of Honor

The bride and groom have decided to marry and have chosen you as their consultant. What now? There are many areas that the couple need advice on. It is up to the consultant to be aware of the various areas that need attention and the traditional as well as non-traditional ways each area can be handled.

One important part of the wedding to consider is the naming of the best man and the maid of honor. Sound simple? It's not. Each of these positions has certain responsibilities that the wedding couple must be able to count on without worry. The consultant plays a part in making sure that the bride and the groom understand these responsibilities and that they choose the person for each position that they can count on. They do not want to choose someone who is likely to back down at the last minute or someone who does not take the responsibility seriously.

Choosing the attendants involves, of course, asking the individuals first. Never let the couple make the assumption that the person they ask will always accept. Usually the choices for best man and maid of honor come from a list of brothers, sisters, best friends, or college roommates. These roles are very special and, therefore, are always a choice of someone very special in the lives of the bride and groom.

It is imperative once this selection is made that the people they choose realize the time and expense involved in the roles. As the consultant, you can play a valuable role on behalf of the bride and groom by explaining the responsibilities of the best man and maid of honor to the people the bride and groom have selected. Before you can do this, you need to help the bride and groom clarify exactly how they want to handle various choices and decisions that must be made about these roles.

Next the bride and groom need to contact their choices for best man and maid of honor to let them know they would like them to fulfill these roles. After these people been have selected, you should plan to contact the best man and maid of honor to discuss some of the unique responsibilities they need to fulfill.

Here are some of the issues that the bride and groom (and their families) need to decide and that you may need to communicate to the best man and maid of honor. One important and costly issue is the question of who pays for the attendants' clothing. In most weddings the groomsmen and bridesmaids will purchase their own clothing, but in some cases the bride's family will pay for these items. Whatever the bride and groom decide, you may need to communicate this to the best man and the maid of honor.

Typically the maid of honor and best man are each responsible for arranging for a gift to the bride and groom from the other attendants. The maid of honor will contact the bridesmaids and arranges for a special, joint wedding gift from all of them. She would also be responsible for collecting money from the attendants and choose a gift they know the bride and groom will love. The groom does the same with the groomsmen. Other brides and grooms may choose not to follow this practice, so it's important that you discuss this with the bride and groom and make sure you understand their wishes.

MoneyMaker Tip: One of the ways you can provide a valuable resource to the bride and groom is to create a list of responsibilities for each, including the average amount of time and money that is spent in the role of both maid of honor and best man.

The temptation is to select best friends and roommates who are not necessarily bad choices, but the burden of playing the honored role of either best man or maid of honor may be more "honor" than some people can afford. It's important to have a frank, open discussion with the bride and groom of the typical practices and customs and the approximate costs of each. If the costs place an undue burden on either the maid of honor or the best man, the bride and groom may choose to modify how they want these things handled. More than one wedding has met near disaster when a party backed out after the gowns were fitted and plans made.

The Role of the Maid of Honor and Best Man

After these requirements are explained to the participants and they accept the positions, the maid of honor typically helps the bride pick out the bridesmaids' dresses, while the best man may assist the groom in choosing the appropriate suits or tuxedos.

The maid of honor will often have a full schedule. If possible she will attend all pre-wedding parties and showers for the bride. Couple's showers are very popular these days, and both the best man and the maid of honor are expected to attend. They often are responsible for planning and arranging for expenses of any bachelor or bachelorette parties.

It is often the case that the maid of honor will help address invitations and make party favors, especially if the couple chooses to do many of these tasks themselves. Of course everything is negotiable and there are few rules cast in stone.

In many weddings, the attendants are responsible for getting the bride and groom to the church on time. They will be available to assist the bride and groom with any help they may need in getting ready for the ceremony. Often best man is in charge of arranging transportation to and from the wedding site, and to the location of the reception and in some cases, to the wedding night location. The consultant may arrange the mode of transportation, such as a limousine, but it is often up to the best man to make sure that everyone is at the transportation location on time.

If there is no ring bearer, the maid of honor and best man are responsible for holding onto the groom's and bride's rings respectively until the clergy or wedding officiant calls for it.

Sometimes the wedding couple will decide that they prefer making honoraria payments to those officiating in the ceremony and to singers and musicians themselves rather than having the consultant do it. Often the bride and groom will ask the best man to present these checks to the clergy or wedding officiant, the organist or other musicians at the wedding site. He does not assume the financial responsibility, but he does deliver the envelopes.

When the ceremony is over and guests have gathered at the reception the attendants will stand in the receiving line with the bride, groom and parents. The best man and maid of honor act as host and hostess at the reception. They cordially greet guests, dance and mingle. It is also typically the responsibility of both best man and maid of honor to deliver a special toast to the newly married couple.

At times, in certain ceremonies, there is something called a "Money Dance," in which guests dance with the new bride and groom and slip envelopes of money to them during the dance. In some ethnic wedding this is done by pinning money on the bride's wedding gown. The best man starts the proceeding by dancing with the bride while the maid of honor dances with the groom.

When it is time to leave for the honeymoon, the best man and maid of honor generally take the lead in decorating the wedding car. Hopefully, this is done with taste. The maid of honor needs to be available if requested to assist the bride in changing from her bridal gown into her going-away clothes. The best man will return his and the groom's tuxedos to the store the next day if they are rented, unless it has been agreed that the consultant will handle this. The maid of honor also looks in on the dressing or changing rooms to check for any forgotten items.

While all these areas of responsibilities belong to the best man and the maid of honor, the wise consultant will follow-up to make sure things happen as they should. With the consultant's help and guidance in explaining each responsibility of the best man and maid of honor, the bridal couple are assured that their wedding attendants will know exactly what to do and when to do it.

The Business of Wedding Consultant

During the course of your business, you will use many different forms and letters as well as other written material. You use sales letters, brochures, flyers, press releases and such to promote and market your business. You have contracts and letters of agreements you use with your clients and independent vendors. You will also send invoices and statement for billings.

Because documents are so important to your business, this chapter is devoted to the documents you will use in the daily operating of your wedding consulting business.

MoneyMaker Tip: Good information, written in a clear, concise and understandable format can make a very positive impression on your client. However, you are cautioned to copy on a high grade of paper, and use a quality copier. Poor photocopies make your business look very unprofessional.

Permission is granted to photocopy the forms in this book.

The Consultant's Checklist

The number of tasks the wedding consultant must manage can be overwhelming, which is of course the reason why people hire wedding consultants. The following checklist can help you and your client keep track of all the important details.

NOTES

_____

_____

_____

_____

_____

_____

_____

_____

_____

CONSULTANT CHECKLIST

Ceremony Site _____   Address _____

Officiant_____   Phone _____

Reception Site_____   Address_____

Caterer_____   Phone_____

Invitations _____

    Contact _____   Phone _____

Calligrapher_____   Phone _____

Florist _____   Phone _____

Baker _____   Phone _____

Rental Equipment _____   Phone _____

Musicians (Ceremony) _____

    Contact _____   Phone _____

Musicians (Reception) _____

    Contact _____   Phone _____

Bridal Gown Store _____

    Contact _____   Phone _____

Bridesmaids' Gowns _____

    Contact _____   Phone _____

Formal Wear Rentals _____

    Contact _____   Phone _____

Decorations _____

    Contact _____   Phone _____

Limousine _____

    Contact _____   Phone _____

Gift Registry _____

    Other Contact _____   Phone _____

Client Contact Form

It is of vital importance that you keep accurate records. Trusting your memory for all the details of several complex weddings, especially during the busy months of Spring and Summer, could lead to some embarrassing situations for you and seriously affect the future growth of your business. You should document all calls, letters, faxes and conversations to or from your clients and vendors. Following are some examples of some tracking forms you can use.

MEETING NOTES

Date:

Contact Name:

Address:

Phone Numbers:

Name of the Bride:

Name of the Groom:

Wedding Date:

Wedding Site:

Customer Comments or Concerns about Wedding Service:

EXAMPLE OF REPORT TO CLIENT
Your Letterhead

Date

Client Name

Client Company Name

Client Address

Dear _____:

I have completed my analysis of the plans you and I discussed for your wedding. Our main emphasis was plan the elegant event you want while carefully managing the costs. I've also identified some additional services we will be able to use at no additional cost to you, as a result of my relationship with some of the service providers.

I've attached a listing of the services and the prices for each one. Once you've had a chance to review this and you've agreed, I will begin working with each service provider.

Until your wedding ceremony is complete, I will monitor your costs and will guarantee that we will stay within your budget. I will report my activity to help keep you informed.

If you have any questions about the budget, please call me at [*your phone number.*]

Thank you for allowing me to work with you on your wedding. I'm confident that it will be an event you will always remember with pride.

Sincerely,

Your signature

Your company name

Invoices and Statements

Getting paid for your services is important. You've worked hard, but you must invoice your clients before you can expect payment. Following are some examples of statements you can use.

Your Company Name
Your Company address
City, State zipcode
Company Phone Number & fax number

INVOICE

INVOICE NO:
DATE:

DESCRIPTION OF SERVICE	AMOUNT
SUBTOTAL	
TOTAL DUE	

Make all checks payable to: *Your company name*
If you have any questions concerning this invoice, call:
Contact name & phone number

Press Releases

Few things are free in life, so when something that is truly free and valuable, you must grab it. The opening of a new business is news and newspapers print news for free. The promotion or addition of staff members is also news and the paper will print that as well. Another event they will publish is the expansion of your business or addition of new services. Here's an example of a news release:

Press Release

Date: [*today's date*]

For immediate release

[*Your name*], President and CEO of [your business name] announced today that she has opened an office in [your town].

[*Your name*] specializes in wedding consulting for couples in [your city]. She stated, "I believe I can help young couples and their families create truly memorable wedding events while saving them a great deal over what they can do for themselves."

[*Your name*] said she plans to conduct two free clinics on the subject: "How To Have The Wedding Of Your Dreams Without Breaking The Bank." A schedule of clinics and other seminars will be published in the [name of newspaper] on [date].

[*Conclude with some statistics about yourself and your business.*]

For additional information, contact: [*your name; your phone number*]

Contracts and Agreements

Contracts are a very important part of your business. You will use contracts in almost every relationship involving your business. A handshake or verbal agreement used to be binding on two people doing business together. Unfortunately this is no longer the safe way to conduct business. You need written agreements to ensure commitments and payments, and your clients will ask for a contract to lock in the promised prices and services. An effective contract works to the advantage of all parties, but it does not need to be a legal document filled with dozens of "whereases" and "heretofores." A contract lays out the terms and responsibilities of both parties.

When you agree on terms have your new client or contract worker sign two copies of your contract. Give them one copy signed by both of you and keep one copy for your files. As you make agreements with vendors, you want to make sure the vendor understands their responsibilities and the compensations they receive for their services. The contract you use will deal with all these facts. Then make sure you pay the vendor fairly and on time. Keeping these people happy will directly affect how well they serve you, which in turn will affect your ability to serve your clients.

As you are interviewing your clients, take notes. When you get back to your office after meeting with your client, review your notes. Then draw up a letter of agreement reiterating the terms you discussed. This letter of agreement gives you and the client a written summary and ensures the two of you understood each other.

Following are some examples of agreements and contracts you can use. It is advisable that you consult with an attorney and have them review these documents for you. These are considered legal and binding, so you need to make sure you are protected as well as possible by these contracts.

EXAMPLE CONSULTING AGREEMENT

INFORMAL CONSULTING AGREEMENT

YOUR LETTERHEAD

Date

Customer Name

Customer Address

Dear _____:

State the purpose of the letter. Then reiterate what you two agreed to.

(List the services you will provide)

State the compensation you agreed upon for your services and the length of the contract you are undertaking together.

State your primary goal.

Ask them to sign and date both copies and return one to you. Let them know that if they have any questions they can call you and give your phone number. Thank them for their business

Sincerely,

(your name)

(your company name)

Accepted: _____

Signature

Date: _____

Example of Formal Consulting Agreement

CONSULTING AGREEMENT

AGREEMENT is made on this _____ day of _____ of 19____, by and between _____ (hereinafter referred to as the "Client") and _____ (hereinafter referred to as the "Consultant").

In consideration of the mutual promises contained in this Agreement, the Client and Consultant agree as follows:

1. *State the time frame of the term of the agreement.*

2. *Outline responsibilities.*

3. Client will compensate Consultant in the amount of _____ for all services provided by the Consultant. Compensation will be made within _____ days of receipt of client's payment to Consultant for consulting services rendered.

4. Client retains the right to review all services and approve all expenses before they are incurred. Consultant will be required to complete and submit records of services performed as specified by Client, but will do so as an Independent Contractor and shall not act as nor be an agent or employee of the Client beyond the scope of solicitor. As an Independent Contractor, the Consultant will be solely responsible for determining the means and methods for performing the service.

5. Either party may terminate this Agreement by notifying the other party in writing at least 30 days in advance of the effective date of the termination.

6. This Agreement constitutes the complete understanding of the parties and supersedes any other prior agreements, and shall be governed by the laws of the State of _____.

CONSULTANT   CLIENT

_____   _____
Name   Name

_____   _____
Address   Address

_____   _____
City, State, Zip   City, State, Zip

Date: _____   Date: _____

Newspaper Wedding Announcement Checklist

The following guidelines for publicly announcing the marriage is a useful checklist for the consultant to make sure the wedding is publicized on a timely basis. Whether this is part of the services you are providing and coordinating, or the bride is handling this, the checklist will help you make sure things are properly handled.

1. Newspapers: Make a list of all the newspapers' names, addresses, and phone numbers.

2. List the lead-time for wedding announcements.

3. Photos should be 8"x10" black and white glossy prints that have been professionally photographed.

4. An information sheet should accompany photos. (Make copies of the form on the following page.)

5. Be sure to include your name and full address on the back of the photo if you want it returned.

6. Make sure to insert cardboard for support and label the envelope "PHOTO - DO NOT BEND."

NOTES

_____

_____

_____

_____

_____

_____

_____

NEWSPAPER WEDDING ANNOUNCEMENT

Newspaper _____ Photograph Included ?_____

Return to:_____

Address _____ City_____ State_____ Zip_____

Editor's Name _____ Release Date_____

Address _____ City _____ State _____ Zip _____

GROOM   BRIDE

Full Name_____

Parents' Names_____

Address_____

Address_____

Schools Attended_____

Special Clubs_____

Military Service_____

Employment_____

Wedding Date_____

Ceremony Site_____

Officiant's Name_____

Description of Bridal Gown (may be obtained where gown was purchased)

_____

Wedding Bouquet Description (may be obtained from florist)

_____

Honeymoon Destination_____

Residence after Wedding_____

other Info:_____

The Marriage License

Although regulations for wedding licenses vary from state to state, this checklist can help direct you. To process the license the bride and groom must:

✔ Apply for your license at least thirty days before the wedding.

✔ Call the marriage bureau (City Clerk's Office) in your city and make notes (below) of the specific requirements of your state.

✔ Both bride and groom must be present to apply.

✔ Be sure to have all of the required identification papers with them.

✔ Some states require up to five days to process a license.

✔ The groom usually pays for the license. (Fee ranges from $10 to $30.)

✔ The license will be valid for between twenty and 180 days. Allow plenty of time.

✔ Remember - getting the license does not mean the couple are married. A civil or religious official, licensed by the state must sign it to be legally valid.

LICENSE CHECKLIST

We both need:

Identification (Driver's License)

Proof of Age (Birth Certificate)

Parental Consent

Citizenship Papers

Doctor's Certificate

Proof of Previous Divorce or Annulment, if applicable

Fee $_____ Waiting Period _____

License valid for _____ days.

Form for Name and Address Changes

The form on the following page is a necessary one that all couples who marry need. This is a form for the bridal couple to use to change their names and addresses on any accounts or legal papers they may need to change. You should provide copies of this to provide to couples when they come in for consultation. It's a courtesy that will be appreciated. During the hustle and bustle of planning, this is often a forgotten item.

Today, many brides combine names by using their maiden names as their middle name, adopting their husband's surname. Whatever decision the couple makes concerning this, it is absolutely necessary that they consistently sign that name on all important items of identification and all legal documents. Some agencies may require that a copy of the marriage license be sent with a written notification.

Places to Notify:

- Driver's License

- Car Registration

- Social Security

- Voter Registration

- Passport

- Bank Accounts

- Credit Cards

- Insurance Policies

- School and/or Employment Records

- Post Offices

- Investments

- Property Titles

- Leases

- Beneficiaries

- Wills

Any time the consultant can assist the bridal couple with small things like this, the more grateful they are and the more you will be remembered to their friends.

Date_____

Dear_____

    We would like to inform you of our upcoming marriage and the changes that will be necessary in our names and addresses.   My account number is_____

_____   _____
Groom's Full Name   Bride's Full Name

_____   _____
Groom's Current Address   Bride's Current Address

_____   _____
City   State Zip   City   State Zip

CHANGED TO:

_____

   Husband's Full Name

_____

   Wife's Full Name

_____

   New Address

_____

   City   State   Zip

AFTER

_____, 19_____

Please send all forms needed to include by spouse on my policy/account.

I can be reached at (   ) _____ if you have any questions.

                 Sincerely,

_____   _____
Groom's Signature   Bride's Signature

Words of Wisdom As You Get Started

The best guide in any business is your own instinct. Somewhere inside you is a little voice that said, "This could be a great way to do what I like and make money doing it." Don't ignore that voice as you build your consulting business. It will say, "These things should be written down," "That is a person I should contact," and "This is something I should be very cautious about." That voice is your business judgment and no outsider can come close to knowing as much as that little voice.

The forms in this chapter, and other forms that appear in later chapters are invaluable in helping you be more effective. They can act as a memory jogger so you don't forget valuable details. They also build your professional image when you have them at hand when a client asks questions. You can also use each of these forms as part of your learning process. Every question and line of the forms is information that you will need to conduct a full service consulting business.

Read the forms over and make sure you understand why they are written as they are and what information they are designed to gather, and then ask yourself, "Why?"

"Why is that information important?"

"Why would anyone need that kind of detail?"

"Why is that question being asked and where will it be used later?"

You are beginning on a very complex business journey. The journey is confusing at first, but the service is fun. The hassles will cause you to question why you are in this business, but the smiles on couples' faces and the paychecks for a job well done, usually off set those thoughts. In the chapters ahead we will take you deeper into different aspects of the wedding.

NOTES

_____

_____

_____

_____

_____

_____

_____

CHAPTER FIVE

MARKETING AND ADVERTISING YOUR BUSINESS

Generating Business

Getting the word out about your business is something you must do to survive in a home-based business. Starting out, you may be working with a limited or small budget. Nevertheless, don't underestimate the importance of promotion and advertising to your business.

Marketing is the means by which you let customers know who you are and what you have to offer them. Since wedding consulting is a service rather than a tangible product, you must work very hard to get your business in front of potential customers.

Because few wedding consultants have a storefront, it will be up to you to find and keep the clients for your business. In this chapter you'll learn some simple, effective, low-cost ways to attract and keep clients. Because clients are so very important to you and your business, the first thing you'll need to learn is how to find them. When you are ready to market your business, you can take several avenues that are both effective and low-cost. These include referrals, networking, word-of-mouth advertising, public relations, direct mail, telemarketing, and direct sales.

When you are ready to advertise, you can advertise using the print media such as newspapers, magazines and flyers. You can also choose to use live media like radio and television. The Internet is the new advertising medium. It should be neither underestimated, ignored nor taken for granted. It affords you possibilities and opportunities found nowhere else. This chapter discusses the avenues that are the most effective for your wedding consulting business.

In order to become successful in the wedding consulting business, you must have a marketing plan. With a marketing plan, you will take control of your future by planning for sales that happen in both the present and also in the future. You will be better able to anticipate continued growth and expanded opportunities for years to come if you build an effective marketing approach to your business. You will also use your marketing dollars more effectively because a marketing plan will help you avoid hit-or-miss approaches to advertising.

Use this knowledge to your advantage. Everything you learn and know about your business helps you sell the client on your ability to provide the best possible service.

Marketing is hard work and takes time, but your business will fail without it. A good rule of thumb is to plan to spend at least one hour a day on average making phone calls and generating your customer base. Even when your business grows, this simple rule will provide you with a continuing stream of business opportunities.

Finding Clients

Never think for a minute that clients will just waltz through your door raining money down on you. Some may, but you can't count on these kinds of clients to make your business successful.

On the contrary, you have to work very hard to keep clients knocking on your door or ringing your phone. Keep in mind, however, that clients are just about everywhere you look. Think about all the young adults in your community. Think about how many of them will be involved in a wedding in the next few years. Many if not all of them can benefit from your services.

Sure, there are businesses right now providing some of the help they will need, but few full-service wedding consultants are available. Most weddings happen by chance, not by design. Nothing is more user-unfriendly than the informal network of wedding services that are offered in your community. There simply is not a good place to stop, shop and drop your cash ... until now!

As most couples become painfully aware, they must cutback on what they want in their wedding in order to stay within a defined budget. And without help from someone like you, they will still spend more on their wedding than they intended while at the same time getting less than the most for their money. They will also turn to family and friends to ask them to handle much of the work that goes into creating the wedding they really want. You as a wedding consultant can help them get more for their money and help them have the wedding they'd like to have. And the wedding consultant is usually overlooked. That's great news for you because this represents a huge untapped market. But they must be able to find you. They have to know that you're there and they have to know how much you can help them with this all-important event. That's where marketing comes into the picture.

What you offer your clients is a way to save money and reduce wedding day hassles. Your business is made of essentially two things, your time and your expertise. The providing of wedding services themselves-the florist, photographer, the caterer-is straightforward. The value you add to this picture is your ability to deliver creative ways to save on those services for the benefit of your clients.

You provide a service that these couples not only need, but that can save them money. The savings you can generate for them pays your fees and also puts money back into their pocket. To get these clients, you need only convince them of these simple facts.

Marketing

Effectively marketing your business is the key to your success. Marketing involves many different areas. These include evaluating your potential client base, preparing how you are going to approach your business and your market, presenting yourself to clients, delivering quality services to your clientele and following up after you finish your services to assure client satisfaction. It also includes analyzing your business success, studying your competitors and surveying your customers.

To begin your marketing efforts, consider your position in the industry and in the eyes of your client and prospects. For those of you just starting out, consider what you want your image with these people to be. Compare your letterhead, correspondence and brochures to others you receive in the mail. How do yours compare to theirs? You always want to make sure the materials you present to existing and prospective clients are professional, distinctive and convey a sense of your stability.

In addition to your print materials, also consider your sales techniques. Always make plans to follow-up on leads and referrals. Refer back to your personal and business goals often. Make sure that your marketing plan is keeping you on track to meeting the goals you set. If it isn't, adjust your marketing efforts to help you meet those goals.

As you are developing your marketing plan, set up strategies and tactics to help you meet your goals. Begin by selecting areas where your strengths are. Choose a couple of broad areas to help you accomplish the goals and objectives for your bridal consulting business. Choose ones that you know you are effective.

Next set up a marketing budget. A good rule of thumb you can use to establish a budget of five to seven and a half percent of your gross sales for marketing efforts. This gives you enough money to work with to implement effective marketing for your business. Any less than five percent usually means you are not investing enough in yourself to sustain long term growth.

As you're budgeting money, also budget in your time. Budget in the amount of time you can feasibly devote to marketing. One of the greatest dilemmas for the small business owner is that it is not possible to market provide services at the same time. If you market you get customers, but once you start providing services, you have to stop marketing and selling. It can be a vicious circle.

Be realistic and budget in time only what you can honestly spend. If you set your expectations higher than you can achieve, you only undermine yourself. For tactics determine who you are going to as target your market. Also decide what you are going to send them: letters, advertising pieces, coupons, etc. Then determine the frequency and amount of each marketing effort you are going to undertake.

For instance, in your direct mail campaign, it's better to send out a limited number of pieces on a frequent basis than it is to send out a large amount on a less frequent basis. You will be able to follow-up on a small number of pieces, but not a large number. Follow-up is a must!

With all your marketing efforts, keep track of which ones are working and which aren't. The best way to do this is to ask the clients who come to you how they learned about you and your services. You can create a log to track this information. Use your computer to set up a database for your marketing efforts. Then you can easily create reports to tell you where your efforts are paying off and where you need to make changes.

Implementing Your Marketing Plan

Once you have your marketing plan established, start implementing it. Give it about three months and then evaluate the results you've seen from that plan. After that time has elapsed, evaluate how well your marketing plan is working, and be honest with yourself. Did you really follow it? Look at specific areas to see what's working for you and what's not giving you the results you want. Then redesign your plan to put more dollars and time into the areas that are showing you positive results.

When you encounter competition, you should stay firm in your resolve to give you clients a fair price for the services you are providing. Do not let the competition control your pricing. You should know what your costs are and what you believe is a fair price. Unless you are losing a great deal of business to a competitor, think carefully about discounting your services. One of the worst things you can do is dread a customer's business because you sold your services too cheap.

That means it's extremely important to keep your overhead costs down. You want to give your clients the best price and the highest quality of service. If you are forced to compete by lowering your prices, try to match your competition's fees and then sell your client on your superior service. Use letters of recommendation and your referral lists to support your claims. Satisfied customers are the best proof you have of the quality of service you provide.

Look closely at your competition. If they have limitations, design your services to fill the gaps left by your competition. Also get familiar with supporting agencies. Use these to find mentors or others that are willing to share information with you about competing directly.

As your business grows, you can set aside more dollars for marketing to give you the opportunity to grow even more. This marketing plan along with your business goals helps you to set targets for your business and lets you gauge your progress toward your goals.

Marketing to the People You Know

As you are looking for ways to start your business, you need to begin with the people you know. On paper, begin a list of all the people you know. Don't forget to include coworkers, both the ones you work with now and ones you've worked with in other companies. Also list supervisors both present and former. Include people you know from industry and trade associations as well as civic and charitable organizations, your spouse's friends, professional contacts, retailers and service businesses you patronize. All of these are potential clients or lead to potential clients. Because you already know these people, you have eliminated one obstacle in your way. The ice is broken, making it easier to talk to them and let them know what you're doing now.

Most of your friends and acquaintances, including your family, want to see you do well. If you have a service they need, they'd rather put their money in your pocket than put it into a stranger's. Even if wedding consulting isn't something these people need, they may refer people they know to you. The important thing to remember here is that a network of contacts æ friends or otherwise æ is essential to the success of your business. Cultivate and maintain this network of contacts.

This brings up the first big question with which every new business owner must wrestle. Do you pay people for business they bring to you? Money invested wisely in this area reproduces itself many times.

Decide with discretion what you will pay for. A lead is not money in the bank, so leads generally do not require any payment. Many people are honored to help and might feel uncomfortable if you offer to pay them. Others will go out of their way to find you business if they can make even a small stipend for each sale you get from their leads.

Once a lead becomes a sale, then it might be appropriate to pay a small percentage for the assistance, especially if they may have other contacts. It is not uncommon to pay 10 to 20% of the income from that sale as a "finder's fee". To maintain your cash flow, you might consider a "trade out" of the finder's fee, offering to exchange services at no, or reduced charges. Constantly remind yourself that 90% of something is better than 100% of nothing!

Cultivate your contacts and be generous where appropriate. Be ever diligent to add to your network of friends, associates and acquaintances. Try not to burn any bridges no matter how unhappy you may be with your current position, company or boss. You never know when someone could be a potential client or could influence a decision to purchase your services.

Everyone you meet is a potential client. Chances are excellent that they know at least one person who will be in the market for a wedding within the next two years. Although everyone can be considered a potential client, that does not mean they will select your services. Be honest and up front with everyone. If you cannot save them money or they have an exceptional resource already, say so. Positive statements about the competition almost always go further than trying to undermine their credibility.

Trust is an important part of building relationships and getting clients. No matter what stage you are in dealing with existing, former or potential clients, never disclose confidential information to anyone about your clients. And once you have a contract with a client, keep that trust by never using their name without first getting their permission.

Referrals

Referrals is probably your single most important marketing resource as a wedding consultant. Once you conduct a perfect wedding while at the same time finding savings for your client, the word of the quality and value of your services will spread very quickly. When you plan a wedding for young adults, it is quite likely that some of the attendants will be planning weddings within the next year or two. If they know how pleased the bride and groom have been, there is a high probability those attendants and friends will ask you to help them with their wedding too. Savings are always good news to people and businesses. While a certain amount of business will come your way as a result of your good work alone, you can increase the value of referrals with a few easy to do steps.

Referrals and "word-of-mouth" are easy to generate and should become an integral part of how you operate your business. It costs you nothing to ask you friends, family and current clients to tell others about you, your service and the excellent job you did for them. One place to start generating referrals is to ask your most satisfied customers to write a letter of recommendation. These letters of referral can pay big dividends when you start calling on big accounts.

MoneyMaker Tip: Frequently people will say they will write a letter of recommendation, but they never get around to it. Draft a "rough copy" of the letter for them, ask them to read it over and make changes where they like. Then make the changes for them and ask them to sign it. This greatly speeds up the process and you get the letter you really need.

When you do save your client money, you are professional in your dealings with them and treat them with courtesy and respect, they will reciprocate by referring others to you. If handled properly and aggressively, referrals can become the heart of your marketing effort and provide you with a steady client base on which you can grow.

But friends, family and current clients aren't your only source for referrals. The people you meet who are also in home-based businesses can be a source of clients for you. This business network is filled with people who know how tough it can be to establish a successful small business and are more than willing to pass on contacts for each other.

Clubs and professional organizations can also be a source of clients for you. The organizations can be both a source of potential clients among the membership as well as valuable source of referrals for you. The important thing to keep in mind is that you must stay public, stay in touch and keep networking. You never know where your next client may come from.

Attending Chamber of Commerce meetings and functions can provide you with a wealth of information, not to mention potential clients. At these meetings and functions you can learn about how business is conducted in your area as well as who conducts it. The professionals that attend these meetings are all potential clients since many of them may be getting married themselves or have grown children who are.

Once you start accumulating a clientele, it's time to consider how to convert them into referrals. Many of them may not need any prodding to refer others to you. It may come automatically from them. No matter how you get referrals from your clients be sure to follow-up with a letter of appreciation or some token of your appreciation for the lead they gave you. Cards or small gifts on their wedding anniversary will promote good will with your clients and show that you remember and care about them.

In addition to the referral letter, another very useful tool is the referral sheet. The referral sheet makes it as easy for satisfied customers to give you information about other potential clients. With two weeks after their wedding, send your client a letter thanking them for their business and telling them how much you enjoyed working with them. Along with this letter, include a customer referral sheet. Make it easy for them: prepay the postage or include the correct postage for them to mail the referral sheet back to you. The following is an example of a referral sheet you can use or you can design your own.

CUSTOMER REFERRAL SHEET

Your Business Name

Address and Phone numbers

Do you know someone who could benefit from my services?

Please use this form to list any couples who might have an interest in the services I offer. You may return this form to me in the enclosed postage-paid envelope. Thank you for your time.

Referred by: _____

Referrals

Name of person to contact:_____

Name of Bride/Groom: _____

Contact Phone: _____

Contact Address: _____

City: _____ State:_____ Zip: _____

Name of person to contact:_____

Name of Bride/Groom: _____

Contact Phone: _____

Contact Address: _____

City: _____ State:_____ Zip: _____

Name of person to contact:_____

Name of Bride/Groom: _____

Contact Phone: _____

Contact Address: _____

City: _____ State:_____ Zip: _____

Moneymaker Tip: Create a small wedding tool kit with your brochure a few easy to understand checklists and your business card. Give them to your satisfied clients, and ask them to hand them out as opportunities arise.

If you want to increase the pace of the referrals you get, you can use more overt tactics. These tactics include educating your customers, inspiring them and reminding them.

Many of your customers think you have all the business you need or can handle. Let them know that you are always ready for more. Educating your clients, your friends and your family lets them know exactly what you do and gives them an idea about who they can refer to you.

Along with educating your clients, you can inspire them to refer others to you. This can take the form of creating an incentive program for referrals. You can tackle this in any number of ways. For instance, you can offer a discount to other family members when they refer others to you, or you can offer a gift of some sort. The gift could be a free lunch or a small token of your gratitude.

If you want to offer a monetary incentive to clients or others who refer clients to you, there are a couple of ways you can do this. One is to offer a flat fee. Pick an amount that won't put a strain on your budget (possibly $15 - $25). Another is to give them a percentage of the fee you receive from the referral. Again, remember not to jeopardize your budget, yet make it worthwhile to those who take the time to refer others to you. A good range of figures to use that are easy to calculate is 5 - 10%. Think carefully about these two incentive fees. Choose the one you like best and use it consistently with all your referrals. The referring people could compare notes at a later date and develop hard feelings. Perceptions of unfairness could damage your reputation.

Another way to inspire clients to help you promote your business is to ask them to write you a testimonial letter. This helps strengthen their commitment to you and gives them a vested interest in your business. It reinforces in their mind that you are in the market for new business and cause them to be more likely to think of you when they meet someone who needs your services. In addition to all this, you now have a solid testimonial to show to potential clients.

All your efforts to get your existing clients to refer others to you won't mean a thing if you don't constantly remind them that you're still in the market for new clients. You can do this by sending out reminder letters on a frequent basis that remind them to refer others to you. You might also offer a gift certificate redeemable for a special "anniversary gift" for their bride and groom if they provide a qualified lead that results in a sale. This will give them a little push to make referrals. Use your imagination and keep in mind what your budget allows for incentives that will entice your clients to help you build your business.

There are many specialty advertising companies that offer catalogs. Use these catalogs to order small, relatively inexpensive items. These companies will print your business name, logo and contact information on these items. Use these as gifts to give those clients who take the time to refer others to you. The gifts you can choose range from fairly inexpensive pens or pencils to calendars and T-shirts.

The important thing to remember is that you want to constantly remind clients that you are in business and that you are always looking for new clients. Don't waste this most valuable of resources. Ask every client you get for referrals.

While you're enjoying all the rewards yourself of getting your clients to refer others to you, make sure that you give these new clients the same care, consideration and professional service you gave those who referred them. Keep your service consistent and the integrity and quality of your work will be the best advertising you could do.

Marketing, A Matter of Image

All the contacts and leads in the world aren't going to help you if you don't know how to present yourself. They also won't help you if you don't take the effort to follow through and make the contact with the lead yourself.

Once you set up appointments to meet with contacts you received through your network or from referrals, you need to present yourself in a positive and professional manner. Always put your best face forward. A positive attitude, enthusiasm and belief in yourself and your services will help to show your clients they are making a wise decision. If you are excited about what you do, your clients catch that excitement.

Here are some specific areas in which your image will shine when you do it with professionalism.

Business Letters

You will more than likely use the business letter as a sales tool. The sales letter can be used to accompany a brochure or other informational material. This method is good for soliciting business and using in mass mailers.

You can also use the sales letter to establish contact with vendors of wedding services after you hear of accomplishments they have made. Another source for potential recipients of your sales letters is engagement announcements in the local newspaper. Sending a congratulatory letter to this individual along with a little information about your service could gain you valuable leads and referrals.

Although generic letters are easy to use, it is advisable to never send out a letter that is obviously generic. Most people toss such letters in the trash without bothering to read them. With the advancements word processors have made in the past several years, there is no need to resort to a generic letter addressed at no one in particular. You can create a letter you want to use for a mass mailer and then set up a mailing list of recipients. Most word processors let you mail merge so that you can address the same letter to a different person. With careful writing, you can create a letter that appears to be quite personal.

Here is a letter you can use to expand your business.

SALES LETTER

Your Letterhead

Date

Contact Person

Address

Dear _____:

Introductory paragraph. Relate this paragraph to your wedding consulting business and the impact it has on it.

Enclosed is a brochure that explains our services. In this brochure you will read about my commitment to quality and how I work with clients. [*Insert Your business name*] works on a contingency basis.

I recently worked with [*insert names of recent clients here*] and helped them enjoy the wedding day of their dreams at a price they could afford. I've enclosed a copy of a letter they wrote to me shortly after they returned from their honeymoon.

I'd like to call you on [*state a specific date*] to see if I can help you plan and conduct the wedding you've always dreamed of.

Thanks for you time. I look forward to speaking with you soon.

Sincerely,

Signature

Your name typed

Wedding Consultant

Your company name

Congratulatory Letter

The society section of your local newspaper is the place to find engagement announcements. Each of these create marketing opportunities for your business. Following is an example of a congratulatory letter you can use.

Your Letterhead

Date

Congratulatory Person's name

Address

Dear _____:

Congratulations on your engagement. I recently became aware of your engagement through the [*name local paper*] and want to take this opportunity to wish you the very best for your future.

We know from experience that planning a wedding can be a very complex thing. Often, with the blending of families, complication and different expectations will surface. All the issues involved-the place for the wedding, the costs, who's going to pay what, the size of the reception-all these things can unfortunately create family problems before the bride and groom have even become a family.

It doesn't have to be that way. [*Name of your company*] specializes in planning a wedding that will make your special day one of the most worry free and positive events in your life. We have the experience and expertise to make this happen.

Because people are different, there are those who prefer to have us handle the whole occasion and others who prefer to do part of the planning themselves and have us do the rest. We can work with whatever your needs are at whatever level you'd like us to be involved. Our recent clients have experienced the wedding they always dreamed of because of our experience in helping them get the most for their budget. I hope you'll review the brochure I've enclosed that explains our services and client satisfaction.

I'd like to call you in a few days to see if we can set up a no-obligation appointment to discuss your needs and wishes and see if we can be of service.

Sincerely,

Your signature

Your business name

A Thank You Letter

When you use the services of other professionals you can also consider them as potential clients. While you should not try to sell them your services while you are meeting with them for theirs (unless they ask), afterwards you can send them a thank you letter that is also a sales letter.

Your Letterhead

Date

Contact

Business Name

Business Address

Dear _____:

Thank them for the time they spent with you and the assistance they gave you.

Indicate that you are interested in using their services in the future and that you will refer others to them when you find there is a need.

Enclosed is my brochure describing the services [your business name] provides. I hope you'll review it and call if you have any questions. If you should want any additional brochures to provide to your customers, please don't hesitate to let me know. I'll be happy to send them to you.

Indicate a day you will call back to see if you can be of service to them or their clients.

Sincerely,

Your signature

Your business name

Marketing Through Other Wedding Service Vendors

Two excellent opportunities for indirectly contacting potential clients is through other vendors of wedding services. For example, one of the first places a new bride-to-be goes is to the bridal shop to begin looking at wedding gowns. Whether she selects her gown at that shop or not, she may be in a state of panic about all the details she's just beginning to face. If you have started networking with these service vendors, they may allow you to leave your brochure where it can be seen easily by their customers. This is even more likely if it is a shop you refer your clients to.

Another good marketing area could be beauty salons. Again leave brochures with their permission on the front counter where people pay for the salon's services.

A good way of building good will with such businesses is referring business to them, and perhaps a small gift at Christmas.

Marketing Your Business through Public Speaking and Seminars

Public speaking is another excellent way to promote your business and expand your network. There are a number of groups looking for an interesting speaker who can give their club or organization good information.

MoneyMaker Tip: When working as a public speaker it is always a good idea to create a handout that everyone can keep. This handout should be packed with useful information, the type someone would want to save. And of course when they save it, they save your name as well. Many people however, lose a great deal of money giving away their normal promotional packets when they are asked to speak to a club. This is expensive and defeats the purpose. Make an inexpensive handout for public speaking audiences and offer additional information if they want it.

Take every opportunity that comes along to speak before groups and organizations and offer public service seminars. When you address audiences be sure to concentrate on their needs rather than your own. You'll be a success and asked to do more appearances. Here's a list of people who might invite you to speak about your business:

- Chamber of Commerce
- Rotary Clubs
- YMCA/Community Action Groups
- Men's Fraternal Organizations
- Women's Organizations and Clubs
- Local church groups
- PTA
- Association meetings

Seminar Sales Letter

From time to time you may want to conduct seminars or clinics in your area. When you do this, you need to market in order to get participants. Of course you will post a press release in your local newspaper, but you also want to send out mailers inviting people to attend. Following are two examples of the types of letter you can use.

Your Letterhead

Date

Contact

Address

Dear _____:

We at [*insert your business name*] would like to introduce ourselves and invite you to attend a seminar on cutting the high cost of weddings. At this clinic we will analyze wedding ceremonies and identify costly mistakes. We will also show you how you can reduce costs by doing certain things yourself. In addition we will also teach you the latest trends in contemporary wedding ceremonies.

The name of your clinic or seminar

location

time

date

seminar fee

We have enclosed one of our brochures for you to review which gives details about our presentation.

Explain the savings you helped others achieve at your last seminar. Justify that the savings make the fee you charge worth the investment.

Please call us at your phone number to reserve a place at the clinic.

Sincerely,

Your signature

Your business name

Public Relations

Your ability to get press coverage has a significant impact on the success of your business. An effective public relations plan can give you in return much more than it ever costs to implement. The key is understanding how the media works, developing the right approach and being persistent.

Treat reporters and editors just like your very best customers. Your best customers became your best customers, because you took the time to understand their needs, to adjust to their schedule and to provide the best possible service. The same applies to the media. Reporters work on tight deadlines. They are interested in good sources who provide timely, accurate information. Respect them and most will respect you.

Start with identifying reporters who you think might be interested in your company. This group might include the society page editor of your local paper as well as the person who handles wedding announcements. Expand the list to include the editors for personnel changes columns, events calendars and syndicated columnists. Ask them how they prefer to receive information, for example, via phone, fax or e-mail. It is your responsibility to make sure you provide accurate information, including spelling of names. Then keep that list updated regularly.

Next, get to know the style and type of stories produced by local media and key reporters who cover your industry, both locally and in this profession. Read their articles and listen to their commentary. Learn their preferences for news releases, backgrounds, photo needs, etc.

Because writers work on tight deadlines, you may only get one call, so respect all reporter deadlines and return every reporter's calls promptly. Provide accurate information, and follow up with a courtesy call occasionally. Build a relationship just as you would with your key customers.

There are many ways to approach the media with a story idea. The simplest method is to write a pitch letter outlining your ideas. Next, you can write a news release and mail or fax it to a reporter. News releases should include a contact name and phone number, suggested headline, a dateline, and the "who, what, when, why and where" of the story idea. Remember to include quotes from your company and third-party sources if possible. However, remember that unless it is a truly significant new story, you probably will have to follow up with a reporter and "re-pitch" the story over the phone. Again, it pays to be brief and treat a reporter like a customer who may or may not want to "buy" your story. Here are some story angles to try:

Singing the praises of your company's services yourself often sounds self-serving to the media. Telling that same story from your customer's perspective adds credibility that the media will notice. An example would be spotlighting large savings that you've netted for a client. This type of article can also be placed in various industry trade publications.

The media also loves to cover trends and issues. Simply by being in the business, you have knowledge of the wedding industry that may help the media cover a trend or an issue from a different perspective. Look for the types of stories the general media is covering. Then think about what is going on in your business. How can you tie the two together? Reporters are always looking for leads and interesting people to interview. Here is a sample news release:

Sample Press Release

August 18, 1997

Recipient's Address

Dear (*Recipient's name*):

(*Your company name here*) has opened an office in (*your town*).

(*Your name*) specializes in Wedding Consulting for couples in (*your city, town or county*).

Their primary goal is:

To assure every bride and groom of the perfect wedding day, hassle free and always the least expensive manner possible.

(*Your name*)'s firm plans to conduct two free clinics on Low Cost Weddings and six seminars this year. A schedule of clinics and seminars will be published in the (*name of newspaper*) on (*date*). Reservations are required and space is limited.

(*Give some vital statistics about yourself as they pertain to your business here.*)

For additional information, contact:

(*Your name and phone number*)

* * *

Adjusting Your marketing Efforts

You've now mailed the press release. You think it is the best you've ever written, and you chose the perfect subject to profile. Yet, no one pays attention to it. You call a list of reporters who feign interest, then back off. At times like these you must remember that persistence is critical. Try a different list of reporters. Rethink your lead. Try a new angle with a reporter. Just don't give up. Few things are free in life, so when something is truly free and valuable, you must learn to grab it! The opening of a new business is news, and papers print news free. The promotion or addition of staff members is news, and the paper will print that information free. The expansion of your business and the addition of new services are also news.

Direct Mail

The mail is one of the best promotional tools you have available. Not only can you use the mail to thank your clients for referrals and remind them you need more, you can use it for another purpose. Use mail as a sales tool to help you build your client base. Create a sales letter that introduces you, your services and offers the prospective client an incentive to give you a try.

As you are out and about meeting people, take note of who they work for, their phone numbers and addresses. Collect business cards from everyone you can. You can purchase a business card rolodex or filing system at any office supply store. Use that to file these cards away for safe keeping until you need them. But before you file them away, set up a database or computerized mailing list/address book with these addresses and phone numbers in them.

By creating an electronic mailing list, you can use it with your word processor's mail merge feature to mass mail sales materials. You might want to set up two lists. One list is for your current clients which you use to send out reminder letters, thank you letters, newsletters, or updates on services you have to offer. The other list is for potential clients. These are the people you meet or that are referred to you. This list you use to send out that beautifully composed sales letter to win them over and add them to your client base.

If your budget allows, there are several direct mailing services with whom you can contract. Some make it possible for you to rent mailing lists from them. Others can provide you with a turn-key operation. These companies offer a variety of services, including mailing to a list of potential customers for you, tracking the results of those mailings and even telemarketing follow-up. Of course the more they do for you, the more they charge.

Mailing lists come in a variety of choices. You can choose a list for a specific zip code area, a certain business type, a demographic group, certain cities or townships, or any other way that people can be classified.

To help you identify the best list to use for your mailing, it's worth contacting a list broker. The broker will conduct a search for you and make recommendations for your consideration. If you've never rented a list of names before, you'll appreciate having them walk you through the process, at least the first time. Look under "mailing lists" in the Yellow Pages to find a broker near you.

In many cities there are businesses that specialize in a similar form of direct mailing. You've seen those thick stock pieces you get in the mail that have the lost children on one side and a business advertisement on the front. You can let these companies design the advertisement for you or you can use your own.

Another form of direct mail is produced by the coupon companies that do monthly mailings, like Val-Pak. Again, you can let them design the coupon for you, or you can furnish your own. Both of these direct marketing companies allow you to choose which areas will receive your mailings. They have residential as well as business lists.

If neither of these options fit within your budget, however, don't despair. You can create your own mailing list. Then you can go to the post office and request a bulk mailing permit. This will entitle to a discount on the postage. With this method, you can create your own letter or advertisement, and you can save money by sorting the mail by zip codes before you deliver it to the post office. This can be time consuming, but the post office is giving you a discount because you're willing do some of the pre-work for them.

Direct mail responses may be slow or seem few in number. Many business people are too busy to read all their mail. Sales literature is often tossed in the trash. A reliable benchmark for response rates is one to five percent. One to two percent is commonly perceived as a significant rate of response. Here's the point. Your direct mail needs to be designed to stand out amongst the clutter in a recipient's mailbox.

It's very important to follow-up your mailings with phone calls. Contact recipients within the first week or two after they receive the mailing so it's still fresh in their mind. Don't sit back and expect them to call you. You must stay on the offensive. Be persistent and don't let poor response distract you. Generating new business is a numbers game.

The sales letter should be used to contact a prospect and set them up for a telephone call from you. In your sales letter don't sound too eager for their business. Play it cool.

Brochures are very important to your business, therefore, you might want to have a professional design one for you. This is one area where you are best advised to have someone else create your work for you. If you are strapped for cash, don't forget, that brochure writer may have a wedding coming up soon. Design and use brochures either in conjunction with or as a follow-up to the sales letter. Your brochures should be informative and easy to understand.

Your brochures should include an explanation of your services, your background and your expertise in a style that's interesting to read. Use these in direct mail campaigns and in your meetings with clients as a way to educate them about your business and services. Your brochure shows the customer the benefits of using your services.

Telemarketing

All the referrals, marketing brochures and sales letters are wasted if you don't follow up. Once you have rented a mailing list, made referral contacts and sent out your letters, you need to contact each person who received the mailing.

The best way to handle this follow-up is with a personal phone call. You may be timid at first, and you may run into a few curmudgeons who try to ruin your day and dampen your confidence. Don't let them get to you. Keep dialing. A good ratio of calls to success is 30 to 1. That's right, 30 phone calls for one decent contact.

The key point is simply, don't stop making those calls just because one person was rude. Take a breather. Walk around. Get a cup of coffee or a soda from the kitchen and take deep breaths to calm yourself. All the while, you should keep giving yourself positive feedback. Tell yourself this was only one unhappy person, and it had nothing to do with you. You have a valuable service that has the potential to save families hundreds of dollars. His or her rudeness is only cause for his or her loss. Be glad you don't have to keep working with them and move on! Then, get back in there on that phone and keep calling those people.

You wasted your money if you don't follow up. Spend as long as it takes to contact everyone to whom you mailed ads or letters. As you're talking to them, be considerate of their time.

Very few people will buy what you are selling on the phone. Your goal is a face to face meeting, not a new wedding contract. Work out a convenient time for the two of you to meet and discuss your services in person. Remember, there is nothing feasible you can do over the telephone. You have to see their family, meet the couple and know what wedding specifics they desire in order to be of value to the client. Therefore, a face-to-face meeting is of utmost importance. It's advisable not to have them come to your home for the initial meeting-it's too dangerous these days letting someone you don't know in your house. After the first meeting, you'll be able to make an intelligent judgment about subsequent meetings.

Direct mail is an excellent way to begin generating new business. Your direct mail flier lets potential clients know who you are and what you have to offer. It gives you a foot in the door. The follow-up you do afterwards opens that door enough for you to meet face-to-face. Once there, it's all up to you to show them the benefits of using your service.

Selling Your Services

Selling is not everyone's cup of tea. In fact many people dread it about as much as they dread going to the dentist. It is, however, one of the most effective ways to generate new business. Once you get over the initial fear of making those "cold-calls," it's really not so bad.

It is important to get in front of the right person, the person who can make the decision to use your services. Talking to anyone else can be a waste of your time and theirs. If the bride's mom and dad are paying the bills, make sure you have her parents in the room. Sometimes you have to go through the couple to get to the pocketbook. In that case get them excited about what your business can do for them and help them focus on exactly what they want. This way they can make a clear case to her parents. As a general rule, aim for the top. If you target the person that ultimately makes the decision, the least you'll get is a referral to a lower level.

Although a little frightening at first, direct sales can generate a good deal of business for you. If you use your time wisely, you will call only after you have made appointments. If you've never been involved in sales or cold-call selling, you might want to start out slow and easy. Drop by a few vendors of other wedding services, and explain to them that you were visiting a client in their neighborhood. Then tell them what you do. Tell them about the possibility that they might also be interested in working with you.

Many people find it easier to talk about the business to a professional and build some confidence before they actually start talking about weddings to young couples. The more you talk about your business the more comfortable you will become. Take advantage of business networking opportunities to make sure you have a clear presentation of who you are and what you have to offer. Remember, when you are making cold-calls, the worst thing that can happen to you is that these people will tell you they're not interested. This won't kill you. It won't even maim you. It might hurt your feelings a little, but it's nothing you can't get past. Just remember, they're not rejecting you, just the profit you offered them.

As you meet people you will begin to amass positive experiences. These positive experiences should be used to reflect on when you're having a particularly bad day. Instead of focusing on the negatives, remember the positives and think about your successes. If you're getting rejection after rejection, don't continue the rest of the day in a negative vein. Go visit one of your existing clients. Just visit with them to help boost your ego again.

You determine where your marketing efforts begin and end. Since you travel to the client, you need to choose how far you are willing to travel: when you start your day and when you end it. Remember, you can perform some of your services over the telephone and via mail. You can extend your market outside your immediate community. You can extend it to cover beyond your city into your whole region, state, or even anywhere in the country.

Advertising

Advertising goes hand in hand with your marketing efforts. It's the way you let the public know about you and your business. There are a number of ways you can advertise. Some of them have already been mentioned æ direct mail, direct sales, and telemarketing, but you can also use other media. These include media such as newspapers, newsletters and magazines. You can use live media such as radio, television and the Internet. Because these are such an important part of developing your business and promoting your image, each is covered in more detail later in this section.

Another part of your on-going advertising and promotion that is equally important is the image projected by your company name, logo, stationary and business cards. It's an area you need to consider. These are things you use in your business almost every day, and they carry a heavy impact. You want them to convey quality, proficiency, thoroughness and professionalism.

For your company name, pick one that conveys the type of business and service you're conducting. Then select a logo that complements this. Use your business name and logo on all your stationary, forms and business cards. What you want is to reinforce with your clients what it is you do so they will think of you when they think of a wedding.

The last thing you want your clients to think about you is that you're an amateur. You are not a "house-wife" trying to start a business; you are a professional who is running a business. The distinction is significant, and must be a part of your thinking. You want your first impression with them to be professionalism and quality, and often your stationary and business card are the first impression they get.

If you lack the talent to do it yourself, you should use a professional writer or designer at an advertising agency or print shop to help you create your company name and logo. Don't be ashamed if you don't have the talent for this. After all this isn't your specialty. Hire someone who has that specialty. If cost is a factor for you, consider using the art department at a local university instead. Many times you can find an undergraduate student to do this for a nominal fee.

While just about any advertising can be good for you, not all the advertising media available are the best option for you. Some work better for certain businesses than do others. This section is meant to be a guide to let you know how to use each of these mediums and which ones are the most effective for your business.

Print Media

Print media come in several forms. Other than what you generate yourself, such as promotional letters, thank-you letters, ad pieces and newsletters, there are newspapers and magazines. Which of these you use depends on the market you want to target. Print media are useless and a waste of money if the people you want to reach don't read the paper or magazine in which you advertise.

When you are creating your brochures, sales letters and other marketing tools, don't attempt to tell everything you know. Provide only enough information to entice the prospective client to want to find out more. The key is to suggest several easy-to-implement ideas to illustrate how much they can save if they use your services. In this business giving clients information they can use is critically important. Even if they do use your information, they still have all the problems to deal with. The more knowledgeable they are, the more likely they are to buy your services.

Your local newspaper or community newspapers can be good targets for your marketing budget. There may even be times when you can take advantage of free advertising opportunities that come your way. Many times certain business activities receive coverage in local or community papers, especially when they relate to community activities. Some papers assign reporters to cover local business happenings and this could be an opportunity for you to have a feature story written about your business. Either of these two events can create opportunities that keep your phone ringing and even lead to long-term commitments.

In the business and classified sections of many of the larger daily newspapers, there are sections where businesses like yours æ small, home-based businesses æ can advertise their services and products at reasonable prices. In community papers these rates may even be lower. Determine which of these papers can offer you the best exposure for the money invested and use them to periodically promote your business.

If your bridal consulting business is located in a small to mid-sized town, you can generate some publicity for yourself by creating a press kit. A press kit consists of articles you can place with newspapers or radio spots to be read on the radio. Announce special events like the opening of your business, the anniversary date of the opening of your business, and wedding clinics you are holding. In this press kit, emphasize your business's unique services: saving couples money on their weddings. Then deliver your press kit to your local newspapers and radio stations.

When you plan seminars or other similar presentations, contact your local and community newspapers to get them to cover your activities. You may have to prepare and furnish your own copy to them. Keep in mind the press is more likely to give you the coverage you need if you don't appear to be self-serving. Present your facts in this light and you'll have more success with the press.

You probably have a number of local, independent publications that are unique to the city or community. Do not overlook these resources as possible markets for promoting your business. Some of these publications target a specific region of the city or focus on special demographics such as families. Others target a special interest group, such as computer users. Get a few copies of these publications and look through the types of ads they carry along with the types of articles they publish.

This gives you a feel for the audience of the publication. If there are no ads similar to your business, you have good news and bad. The good new is you may have a new and untouched market. The bad news is, if no one else is using the media, it may be that it doesn't work for your type of business. The key here is to determine what the audience is for a particular publication and then target your marketing at that group. Do your homework and research each publication you are considering. Learn the habits of your potential customers. What are young couples reading? Where do they get their information about weddings and how do they select the services they want?

When creating any written materials for your business æ press releases, letters, brochures, ads, etc. æ include the five "W's": who, what, when, where and why. These are the basic rules of journalism and are proven to work. They give readers everything they need to know. Get your readers involved at the beginning of your material and personalize the information to them. Put your most favorable information at the beginning and also the end of your material. Always present your material in positive terms and gear your style to your readers.

Live Media

Live media includes radio and cable and broadcast television. While these are good media for most advertising, they may not be the best for your business, or your budget. The money you spend for this type of advertising is quite high, and the results may not equal the amount you have to spend. Radio and local television stations are excellent for press releases announcing the opening of your business or the clinics you are holding in your community. Television and cable run 30 or 60 second spots or ads about your business. You can also use these to promote your clinics; however, the cost may not be feasible. In order for these media to work you need to run many ads over a length of time. Studies have proven that the most effective ads are those that inundate the public with information. Doing this can be quite expensive.

MoneyMaker Tip: You may have a public interest slant that can be run at Valentine's Day or during the peak wedding months. Be creative and work with the local reporters. They are looking for your information. If you are a storehouse of interesting wedding tidbits, someone will run it on the news, and that's for free.

If you feel you want and need to use either of these media to promote your business, you may be able to get a business loan to cover the expenses of this type advertising. Or you can wait until your business is generating enough revenue and profits to warrant this kind of expenditure. Usually small businesses get better results, especially when they are starting out, by using direct mail, telemarketing, referrals and direct sales.

The Internet

The Internet offers a number of ways to promote your business. It also lets you reach people not just in your own back yard, but across the globe as well. This astounding medium lets you operate a business 24 hours a day, 7 days a week, to almost anywhere in the world. All this can be done without your being there round the clock. Anything you can do with print media, including direct mail and newsletters, can also be done on the Internet. For a relatively small amount of money you can have a web site designed for you. The Internet and the World Wide Web allow you the flexibility to create a full color display of virtually anything you want. If you haven't already connected, take a look around at what is being done and how others are using the Internet to increase their business exposure to find more clients.

The Internet is composed of several different areas. Some of these are only useful to you for research purposes, but many of them are useful to you for promotional purposes as well. For the purpose of this section, we only cover the promotional avenues of the Internet and on-line services.

E-mail lets you communicate with clients quickly and inexpensively. It can also be used to send direct mailings to clients and potential clients. Bear in mind, however, that certain types of advertisements are considered bad manners on the Internet. You must do your homework and check the "FAQ" sheets posted by many newsgroups to find out what's appropriate and what's not. To make the Internet work for you, you need to set up your own mailing list of contacts.

Newsgroups like **misc.entrepreneurs and misc.business.consulting** are another good communication tool at your finger tips. These groups, or forums as they're called by on-line service providers, are excellent sources of information as well as potential resources for clients. There are thousands of newsgroups you can join, and they're free! Look through the list your Internet service provider offers you and select some that are related to either home-based businesses or to the wedding services industry, or both. Monitor the postings or messages for awhile to get a feel for the groups. Then as you can, answer questions that are posted.

Use your signature line. Remember, it's like your letterhead only in reverse. It appears at the end of your postings automatically after you set it up and can contain anything you want like your business name, logo, address, phone numbers, e-mail address, web page address and so forth. As you answer questions, it lets the others in the group know who you are and what you do. After time you'll start getting private postings asking you to give them more information about what you do. This is an opportunity to sell your services. You can also add these people to your mailing lists. If they ask you for information, they are receptive to your sending them advertisements and promotional material.

E-mail has a tool that is similar to newsgroups. These are called mailing lists or "list-serves." These are groups of people with similar interests that form a list to discuss topics of interest to them. Refer back to the previous chapter for a more detailed description of list-serves and examples of some of those lists. When you join them, follow the previous instructions for newsgroups. You'll get the same results.

Chat channels are another excellent communication tool. On the larger nets for IRC (Internet Relay Chat), 20,000 people are on-line at any given time. These people all join various channels or rooms. Some are set up by age groups, some by hobbies, some by professions and so forth. Look through a list and find a channel or two you think might have either an interest in your service, or represent a demographic group you're targeting. Join in the conversation and become accepted as part of the group. Becoming accepted as part of the group can take only a little while or it could take days, depending on how much you like to talk and how receptive the channel is that you joined. On the whole the chat groups are a very friendly and accepting group. Once you establish a bond, you can ease into the conversation what it is that you do. Eventually, you will find people interested in your business. Again, add these to your mailing list and send them information. Of course, go ahead and talk to them, just as though you were talking to them on the telephone or even in person. Use your professionalism to sell yourself and your services.

The most powerful marketing aspect of the Internet is the World Wide Web (WWW). This is where you can create an image for yourself. By creating your own pages and putting them on the Web, you offer your services to people all over the world. Anyone who can access the Internet and the WWW, can access your business pages at either no cost or low cost to you.

There are several options for establishing your presence on the Web. You can take the time to learn how to create and design your own pages, or you can hire one of the many Internet consultants to do this for you. Either way, this is an avenue you should pursue. Web Page Designers for Business is one such consulting company. You can view their pages on the Web at http://www.getset.com/.

There are hundreds more you can find on the Web by doing a keyword search for "web page designers." The fees these designers charge range from $250 for a basic site design to much more depending on what you want your pages to do and how you want them to look. These vendors generally quote on a per job basis.

The nice thing about using these companies is that you don't have to use anyone local. You can use anyone anywhere in the world. The Internet allows information to be exchanged between you and the designer without ever meeting face-to-face.

The cost for marketing on the Internet is relatively low and the potential is very high. The cost to you for Internet business marketing is (1) your on-line connection cost (between $10 and $40 per month), (2) what your provider charges you to hang your business pages (usually a monthly fee and sometimes a usage fee), and (3) what it costs you to have the pages designed (between $50 and thousands of dollars depending on the company you use and how you want your pages designed).

Building Goodwill

As part of marketing and building your business, you also want to establish and build goodwill. Goodwill has a market value to you and for your business. You promote goodwill by thanking people when it's appropriate. You can use letters to thank those who send you referrals, clients who give you their time even if they chose not to use your services, and any other professionals who spent time passing their wisdom and experience on to you. Thank the manager of the facility where you hold meetings or seminars and thank your customers. Show your appreciation to everyone who helps you build and keep your business going. Goodwill also includes community activities, charity work, contributions, volunteer work and promoting special groups.

Take what you've learned in this section and determine where your marketing and advertising dollars will be best spent. Then develop and implement your advertising using the resources that best serve your purposes. Your advertising and marketing costs can get out of hand very quickly if you don't plan and budget for them. Use the guidelines set forth in this chapter to help you plan for the success of your business and to help you increase your client base. You should always know how much you plan to spend, how well it is working and what you are planning next.

The Outlook for Wedding Consulting

The outlook for wedding consultants is brighter today than it was a few years ago. At the time, the trend was toward small informal weddings. People gave weddings without outside help. Now many brides and their families are working and do not have the time to plan a formal wedding, which can be very complex and time-consuming. The mobility of many people in the United States has contributed to long-distance weddings. Participants from far-away regions make planning even more difficult.

There are several new trends occurring in weddings, and this field is nearly recession proof. More people marry each year, and the number of larger weddings is increasing. People are spending more on flowers and dresses for the wedding, for the receptions, and for honeymoons farther away. The traditional church wedding with six or more bridesmaids is coming back. There are more second marriages that require consultants, as well.

Independent wedding consultants may earn very little when they start to build a business. They may earn a great deal more as the business grows and they become well known. Those who cater to an exclusive clientele may earn $100,000 or more a year. The first year, a wedding consultant should anticipate earnings around $25,000. Motivation determines how high you go. Increases of eight to ten percent each following year should be expected.

The IRS and Wedding Consulting

One extremely important point to remember and keep in mind at all times is this: Don't forget taxes! Not only taxes, but, there are many more financial aspects to remember that independent consultants often forget, especially at the beginning. Like all other small business owners, wedding consultants need to keep records of their costs and income. When you are self-employed, you must set aside stated times to review your business to learn what activities are resulting in profits and which activities you should change to improve business. You have to continuously cultivate sources that offer cost-effective, reliable, quality services. Also because you own your own business and are self-employed, you must provide your own medical insurance and retirement savings.

You must also consider the time and expertise it will take for doing your own bookkeeping, buying, marketing, advertising, and all other actual business aspects. It is vital to do your best to keep overhead down. This means you should try to perform as many job functions as you can on your own. But, you have any confusion at all about your finances and taxes, do not hesitate to hire an accountant. This may be the one person who keeps you in business. Once you learn all there is to know about the business, you can then decide what aspects of the business you want to tackle, and there are many. With experience, you will also learn how to save the bride money. You'll learn where to cut costs without sacrificing any of the beauty or elegance of the wedding.

For More Information on Training and Setting Up Your Business:

The National Bridal Service consists of owners of bridal stores (apparel stores and bridal gift registries). This group works to increase the quality of bridal store management and employees. It conducts seminars and training sessions on topics such as advertising and inventory control. The National Bridal Service also awards the title Registered Bridal Consultant to those who complete the Wedding Beautiful home training course. The consultant must be employed by a store that is a member of the National Bridal Service. Weddings Beautiful, a division of the National Bridal Service, is an organization for wedding coordinators. Coordinators direct wedding rehearsals, assist at weddings and receptions, and do the legwork for bridal activities before the wedding. The title Certified Wedding Specialist is awarded to those who complete a thirteen-assignment home study course and pass an exam.

The Association of Bridal Consultants is made up of independent bridal and wedding consultants and by employees of wedding-related businesses. This group offers a professional development program and seminars on the wedding business. It also offers advertising, publicity, referrals, and information services to its members. Another organization, June Wedding, Inc., also offers a training program.

CHAPTER SIX

ENSURING WEDDING DAY SUCCESS

Suggestions To Please The Guests

Do you have a favorite Aunt Jane? Or maybe an Old Uncle Joe? People who are very special to you? So do your clients, but often these special people are unintentionally left out of the wedding planning process, or they are included only as an afterthought. A professional wedding consultant makes sure all aspects of the wedding meet the couple's needs, including those "special people."

The following are suggestions to offer the bride and groom to help their relatives, guests, friends and themselves enjoy the wedding much more, and look back on it later with very fond remembrances. Many times, it's the little things that mean a lot.

The ideas in this chapter may not make you a great deal of money, but they will make the wedding a special day. And, any one of these ideas could be one of the best investments you make. Don't ever forget, each relative, and friend of the family could represent another wedding.

When you include these thoughtful extras, you will be thanked for your kind consideration. You also may make the lasting impression that results in one of those special people saying, "You made that wedding so perfect for me, I just had to have you manage my own wedding."

And just think, "Uncle Bud" just might be an eccentric millionaire who is getting ready to marry off his only daughter.

Here are nineteen tips for making a fairy tale experience come true for your customers.

Idea One

It's important to make sure that all those "special people" in the lives of the bride and groom are remembered. More than one wedding has been spoiled because a friend or relative felt slighted by not being included.

If you create a "Friends and Family Worksheet," no one will be forgotten. More names will end up on the worksheet than the bride and groom will ever include, but by starting with every possible friend and relative, no one will be left out who should be included in the wedding invitations.

If you then ask the couple to classify the "Friends and Family Worksheet" by different levels of involvement, you can further secure the confidence of the bride and groom in your services. This is a good time to demonstrate the open and honest approach you will adopt as their wedding consultant. Encourage them to frankly discuss the personalities and habits of each person on the list.

Some people are comfortable out front where wedding guests are and others are much happier behind the scenes, working with the caterer for example. Some people only want to be remembered and do not want or expect to be a part of the wedding. Others will expect to be treated special but will not provide much help.

This conversation is critical to the overall success of the wedding, but it is difficult for most brides and grooms to deal with. Your gentle, outside perspective approach, helping them make an assessment of the facts is invaluable to them.

Family & Friends Worksheet

Name	Level of Involvement		Wedding Responsibility
	Low	High	
_____			_____
_____			_____
_____			_____
_____			_____
_____			_____
_____			_____
_____			_____
_____			_____
_____			_____
_____			_____
_____			_____

Name	Level of Involvement		Wedding Responsibility
	Low	High	

_____

_____

_____

_____

_____

_____

_____

_____

_____

_____

_____

Idea Two

An advanced announcement is sometimes sent to people who are very close to the bride or groom. Ideally this communicates that the bride and groom are thinking of them in a very special way. A sample of an advanced announcement follows. This, along with a special note from the bride or groom can be sent to everyone on their list of friends and relatives.

SAMPLE ADVANCED ANNOUNCEMENT

ADVANCED ANNOUNCEMENT

Name of the Bride & Name of the Groom

We wanted you to be among the first to know about our up coming wedding.

In the next few months the date will be set, and formal announcements will be sent out with all the details, but we wanted to share our initial excitement with you. We look forward to sharing our wedding day with you.

MoneyMaker Tip: Have a preprinted advanced wedding announcement ready at your first meeting with the client. This way you can easily show them what you are talking about when you discuss this idea with them. You may offer this for free, charge a small fee for the advanced announcements or actually contract to handle the mailing of this for the bride and groom.

Idea Three

How many times have you been at a special occasion and at the most inopportune time a zipper pops or a button drops off? At almost every wedding someone will need a Band-Aid and another will look high and low for an ink pen to sign a card. The more people invited to the wedding the greater the likelihood that someone will need emergency supplies, but in a strange place or in the middle of the reception, those items are often hard to find. Your forethought can be a lifesaver.

Have a care package ready at the church, and the reception, complete with stockings, nail polish, aspirin, lipstick, needles and thread. And this is only a partial list. Just think of all the things you've needed when you were at a wedding, or similar event. This prevents on-the-spot set backs from becoming major disasters.

Make sure you let the right people know that this package is available, or no one will know it's available. Almost every family has one person who is the care-taker, someone who naturally nurtures and cares for the little details. By learning the names of the "special people" you will know who to tell about the kit.

The great news about this idea, is that if no one needs it, you are out little if anything. But on the other hand, you have demonstrated how prepared and concerned you are for everyone at the wedding.

MoneyMaker Tip: Many businesses will provide samples and packaging at no cost items for your care kit. By compiling a number of samples, and spending very little money, you may be able to create a number of "care packages." If you include some information about your services in the care package, you can very passively market your business and tell people at the wedding who is orchestrating all the details.

Idea Four

As the wedding draws near, the stress will mount. Even when the wedding is being planned by a first class consulting service, it is easy for the bride to become frustrated and edgy. One way you can provide fun and relaxation is to treat the maid of honor and the bride to a joint make-up consultation before the wedding.

Such a makeover is almost always free. Keep in mind, that this must be scheduled in advance. A good rule of thumb is to plan at least four weeks in advance for this service.

MoneyMaker Tip: By building a business relationship with cosmetic consultants you and they build a clientele that is good for both businesses. It's a great source of referrals for you and them. In exchange for putting the cosmetic consultant in contact with your clients, they will usually hand out your business card or flyers.

Idea Five

Just exactly what kind of gift does the groom give the ushers and his attendants? This is always a difficult decision. Novelty companies have sprung up in great numbers in the last few years, and each has a catalog they are willing to provide a busy wedding consultant.

One very popular item is to suggest that the groom give engraved beer mugs to the ushers. Most novelty catalogs have a wide variety of different and unique mugs available. They are almost always a hit and it takes care of having to worry about individualized gifts.

Idea Six

One of the most effective ways to instill confidence your in services is to build on the memories of special friends of the bride and groom. Here is one way you can become endeared to the friends of the bride and groom and make their special day perfect. Mail a form to all the "special people" asking for their special memories of the bride or groom. You might want to include this memory worksheet with the advance announcement mentioned in Idea Two.

List these memories, along with the name of the person who mentioned each one, in an inexpensively bound small booklet. These you can use at bridal showers, for table conversation, or as part of dedications during the reception. With today's desktop publishing capabilities, it is easy and inexpensive to make a very professional booklet. People like seeing their names in print, and the "special people" like being associated with the bride and groom on this special day.

SPECIAL MEMORIES WORKSHEET

Instructions: Please help make the wedding day of [*insert name of bride and groom*] by sharing your memories below.

Name : _____ Phone: _____

1. What is your first memory of [insert the name of the bride or groom]?

2. Do you have a funny memory or story of your relationship with [*insert name of bride or groom].*

3. Do you have a favorite story from your wedding you'd like to share with the [*insert name of bride and groom*]

4. What is your favorite song from your wedding?

5. What advice or words of wisdom do you want to share with [*insert bride and groom*]?

Idea Seven

One of the most interesting phenomena of a wedding is the memories the wedding evokes for the people who attend on this special day. Moms, dads, aunts and grandparents all have fond memories of their own special wedding day. The sound of the church organ, the wedding march and the pageantry all provoke fond emotional ties to the past. If you have used the "Special Memories Worksheet" you will have the information you need to ask the band to play these favorite songs and use it as part of a dedication dance. Playing special music makes people feel special and adds variety to the reception.

Idea Eight

With today's technology, almost everyone has a tape recorder or at least has access to one. You can make a recording of the memories and thoughts special friends and family members have of the bride and groom. Then give the recording to the couple as a special gift. This can easily be done if you begin several months before the wedding.

This idea works similar to a chain letter. Using the list of special people, send the tape to the first one on the list asking them to record a message and then send the tape on to the next person on the list. Make sure you assign a deadline to ensure that the tape returns to you by the deadline. To speed up the process you might start several tapes at once.

The people who participate in this tape have a great deal of anticipation and look forward to participating in creating this special gift. This builds anticipation for the wedding and results in a very special keepsake. In fact, copies of this tape can easily be sold for $10 each, which will more than compensate for the time and development.

Sample Tape Routing Slip

Directions: Enclosed is a cassette tape. We are creating a special, surprise gift for [*insert the name of the bride and groom*]. Please record your best wishes, advice or special memory (no more than 2 minutes please), cross your name off the list below and then mail the tape and these instructions on to the next person on the list.

Name	Complete and Mail By
1. _____	_____
2. _____	_____
3. _____	_____
4. _____	_____
5. _____	_____

Idea Nine

Few things are colder than an empty hotel room, and few things make a person feel more remembered and welcome than a nice gift basket waiting in their hotel room. You might also include an agenda for the wedding activities along with special directions to the church, reception and restaurants.

Idea Ten

In larger cities, a map with specific directions can be very helpful to people who are not familiar with the territory. Special phone numbers and the names of wedding guests from the other side of the party can also be helpful to the families of the bride and groom.

The full service wedding consultant has access to all the contacts and information needed to complete the suggestions above. With just a little forethought, these can be done for almost no cost and little time, but the good will generated is enormous.

By the way, don't forget to have the name of your business attached.

MoneyMaker Tip: Create out-of-town wedding packets that include hotel information, maps and complete directions to the church and reception hall. Usually the Chamber of Commerce will provide these to you for free. For weddings held out of town, or weddings that have a high percentage of people traveling in from long distances, this service is very important. Included in this information can be limousine or transportation options.

Idea Eleven

A thoughtful idea for place cards in a small wedding is to use antique looking miniature picture frames. They can be then kept as a remembrance. If this becomes cost prohibitive, provide these for the bride and groom's "special people."

Idea Twelve

If the honeymoon doesn't start right after the wedding, suggest that the newlyweds host a post reception party for the long-distance guests who remain in town. It will help pass the time until the couple leaves on their honeymoon, too.

Idea Thirteen

For bridesmaids' gifts, suggest that the bride give jewelry that she wants them to wear at the wedding. Other ideas are personalized address books, stationery, compact silver mirrors, lingerie bags, picture frames, maybe a trip to a beauty salon or even glamour shots.

Idea Fourteen

It's a good idea to send out schedules a few weeks ahead of the wedding, letting the wedding party know where and when they are needed, such as at the rehearsal and picture taking sessions.

Idea Fifteen

Have the guests sign the matting around a large print of the couple's engagement photo. This makes a wonderful, sentimental memento for the bride and groom.

Idea Sixteen

To save on flowers, bridesmaids might carry Bibles instead. These can be dedicated to each member of the bridal party and signed by the bride and groom. This idea isn't for everyone, but in some cases can be a very special touch.

Idea Seventeen

Help the bride and groom start a newsletter to keep family and friends up on all the news since the wedding. This newsletter can be kept up indefinitely and keeps everyone connected in a special way. Make up copies of samples in advance and give them to the bride and groom to give them ideas. This also can be a special service your consulting business provides, if you happen to be a writer.

Idea Eighteen

And, you, the consultant, should make sure that the caterers set aside a basket of goodies for the bride and groom, since they may not have much time to eat at the wedding. They will be circulating the room, greeting guests and family members. It would be a shame if they missed their own reception dinner.

Idea Nineteen

Instead of just having a beautiful wedding cake, some brides are also providing a groom's cake as well as a bridesmaids' cake. The groom's cake is usually decorated with the appearance of a tuxedo or something suggestive of the groom. Of course, this cake should definitely be kept in good taste. (Pardon the pun.)

For the bridesmaids' cake, here is a wonderful idea that was used in medieval times and is appropriate still today.   The tradition behind this cake is fascinating and can be lots of fun. Years ago, when a bride would be hidden from her groom during the last few days before the wedding, the husband-to-be would supposedly bribe the bridesmaids with trinkets to let him see his beloved before the ceremony. From this tradition came the Bridesmaids' Charm Cake, also called a Trinket Cake.

From the outside, the cake looks like any other two-layered cake. But, tucked away inside the frosting between the layers are hidden treasures: tiny trinkets with different brightly colored ribbons attached that come out in long silken waves from the inside of the cake. Each bridesmaid pulls a ribbon to extract the trinket that will become theirs.

Many of the trinkets used in the past held a symbolic meaning. An anchor signifies the promise of adventure for the lucky recipient. The coveted ring means that the bridesmaid will be the next to marry. The ribbons should be color-coded: pale pink for singles, white for married, hot pink for the junior bridesmaids. Any flavor or type of cake and frosting can be used. The charms, made of silver, can usually be purchased for about $8-$10 each. The bride can make up the symbolism to match whatever she chooses.

These suggestions are only that - suggestions. Pick the ones you are most comfortable with and give them a try. The purpose of these ideas is improved service, and, if followed, they can certainly make the wedding even more special for the family, attendants, and guests. They can also build a more positive reputation for you and your business.

NOTES

_____

_____

_____

_____

_____

_____

_____

CHAPTER SEVEN

HANDLING THE WEDDING COSTS

How Do You Determine Fees?

When it comes to fees, there are few hard and fast rules. When all is said and done, people hire you for three basic reasons:

1. You have knowledge and information that can help them with their wedding, and they are willing to pay for that knowledge.

2. You can reduce their hassles and wedding day difficulties, and they are willing to pay for that peace of mind.

3. You can save them money by finding discount resources, and they are willing to pay for that savings, assuming your fees are at least off set by the savings.

In most high paying professions, you must study for years, getting an education and a degree in order to demand the money you are worth, but almost everyone will tell you that they learn the majority of the skills by trail and error. Often more errors than one would like to admit.

The good news about wedding consulting is that education is not mandatory and most of the services you will provide as a wedding consultant can be learned as you go. And there's no significant capital investment required to get started. This business is built on your knowledge.

Knowledge is the basic equity your business will build on. So before we go on, let's make sure you understand what you are selling when your primary business product is intellectual equity.

When you go to a doctor for an operation, you receive two things, the actual surgery, and the knowledge the doctor possesses. The fees for the surgery are substantial, but you pay a lot more for what the doctor knows. You are paying for the knowledge and experience obtained through all those years of medical school and "the practice" on all those patients.

The attractive income that a doctor earns comes as a result of a number of years of "practice" and experience. When you pay a doctor for services, about 85% of the bill is based the doctor's knowledge and about 15% of it is based on actual service costs.

Now we're not suggesting that you will charge as much as a doctor for your knowledge, but the concept is similar. Wedding consulting is built on knowledge, and the services are offered in concert with that knowledge. You are paid not only for what you "do," you are paid for what you know. You are of greater value to your clients when you know more about the wedding and the possible services that might be needed.

Today, we live in the information age. In a computer-oriented world, information has become so important that it is possible for people who have never before commanded high wages to receive them based upon what they know.

The good news for you is that wedding consulting fees are still being defined. The marketplace has not set hard and fast numbers on them, so you have greater freedom to decide what price you will set on your time and your knowledge. If your fees are higher than a client will pay, you can adjust them. If your business expands a great deal, you can raise your prices and make people pay for all the knowledge you have now attained.

As a wedding consultant, you must constantly remind yourself of this basic fact: the value of the service comes from the knowledge of the consultant. As a wedding consultant, you may find yourself draping crepe paper in a reception hall or cleaning up a church kitchen because someone forgot to tell the custodian about the reception. Either way you will be paid not so much for what you do, but for the knowledge of what it takes to make a wedding a perfect day.

Clarifying Who Pays the Bills

When it comes to determining who will pay for what on your bill, there are no absolute rules. You do need to exercise some control in this area, however, so that the issue of paying for the different areas of a wedding will not turn into a battle among families. It is important for you to have a clear understanding of this issue so that you can deal with it professionally and with sensitivity.

The following list indicates the traditional assumption of expenses. It is recommended that you provide this list, and then talk about the couples' plans for handling each expense and whether they wish to make different arrangements. It is always easier to talk about costs before conflict arises. Professional wedding consultants learn very quickly in their business development that open frank discussion is better than letting this subject slide.

Early in your work with the couple (and sometimes, with their families), it's best to present a budget and help them discuss who will be responsible for each expense. This will decrease the likelihood of having misunderstandings or hard feelings later on. Wedding expenses are traditionally divided as you will see in the list that follows, but as you will learn early in your work in wedding consulting, each one is different.

In today's society, more and more couples are choosing to handle much of their wedding expenses on their own, relieving some of the financial burden on their families. Therefore, the traditional divisions of expenses may not hold true for each couple. Many couples don't feel that it is "fair" that the bride's family be responsible for so much of the expense than the groom's family.

The groom traditionally pays for ...

✔ His bride's wedding ring

✔ A special wedding gift for the bride

✔ The marriage license

✔ Gifts for the best man, groomsmen and ushers

✔ Certain flowers including ...

His bride's bouquet and going-away corsage

Corsages for mothers

Boutonnieres for the male attendants

✔ Accommodations for out-of-town groomsmen and ushers

✔ His own physical examination

✔ Gloves, ties or ascots for the men in the wedding party

✔ Fee for the person who officiates at the wedding

✔ Honeymoon costs

✔ The bachelor dinner.

Traditionally, the bride is responsible for ...

✔ The ring for the groom

✔ A personal wedding gift for the groom

✔ Presents for the bridal attendants

✔ Personal stationery and invitations

✔ Accommodations for her out-of-town attendants

✔ Her own physical examination.

It is best to provide a copy of the traditional expense divisions to the couple and let them decide for themselves. You should offer information, but never insist that this is the only way it will work.

As you compare the lists above, the financial responsibilities of the bride and groom appear fairly equitable. As you will see in the following lists, however, there is quite a discrepancy between what the bride's family pays for and what the groom's family pays for.

Here how wedding costs have been traditionally distributed:

The bride's family pays for ...

✔ The reception, Beverages & food

✔ Wedding cake

✔ Gratuities for the bartenders and waiters

✔ Decorations

✔ Music

✔ Flowers

✔ A special wedding gift for the newlyweds.

✔ The bride's wedding attire and trousseau

✔ Invitations, announcements, and mailing costs

✔ Both the engagement and wedding photographs.

Additional expenses include...

✔ The cost of the complete ceremony including rental of sanctuary or other marriage site, fees for organist, soloist, choir and music

✔ aisle carpets & Canopies and tents

✔ Bridesmaids' bouquets

✔ Gratuities to those directing traffic as well as parking costs and valets

✔ Transportation for bridal party to the wedding ceremony and from ceremony to reception.

✔ The bridesmaids' luncheon.

The Groom's family is responsible for ...

✔ Travel expenses and hotel bills his family may incur

✔ A wedding gift for bride and groom

✔ The rehearsal dinner.

No matter who pays for what, be sure to include taxes and gratuities in your budgeting. If not, you and the couple will be in for a very unpleasant surprise of hundreds of dollars!

Your role as consultant is to prepare a Wedding Costs List for the bride and groom, review the list with them, and facilitate their consideration of these expenses until they reach the final decision about how the costs will be covered. You will need to help everyone understand that although there is some tradition about payment of expenses, they are not binding. The important thing here, is to help people communicate and reach an understanding about whatever they plan to do .

One way to help the couple determine their costs and establish a budget for these costs is to create a list of the different costs to help them make the best decisions. An example of a Wedding Cost Worksheet, is shown below. On this sheet are columns for you to indicate four different cost levels.

Level One is considered high end products and services

Level Two is the average amount that is spent for this service

Level Three is the economy service, which should be emphasized that this not "cheap." It is just a scaled back version of services.

Level Four is the lowest level of services, which you won't use and may decide not to include on your worksheet.

By providing these levels of costs, you will help the couple control their costs and better understand what is involved in each service.

It is important for you to provide descriptions of the vendors and the levels of service so they can make the best decision possible. You are providing this information so the couple can make an informed decision. The information you are providing justifies why the couple has contracted with you. The more specific you can be, the clearer their decisions will be to them.

THE WEDDING COST WORKSHEET

The Bride's Traditional Responsibilities

Service	Level 1	Level 2	Level 3	Level 4	Total

The ring for the groom_____

A personal wedding gift

   for the groom_____

Presents for the bridal

   attendants_____

Personal stationery

  Accommodations for her

  out-of-town attendants_____

Her physical exam_____

Groom's Traditional Responsibilities:

Service	Level 1	Level 2	Level 3	Level 4	Total
His bride's wedding ring					
A special wedding gift for the bride					
The marriage license					
Gifts for the best man, groomsmen and ushers					
His bride's bouquet and going-away corsage					
Corsages for mothers					
Boutonnieres for the male attendants					
Accommodations for out-of-town groomsmen and ushers					
The bachelor dinner					
His own physical exam					
Gloves, ties or ascots for the men in the wedding party					
Fee for the person who officiates at the wedding					
Honeymoon costs					

The Bride's Family's Traditional Responsibilities:

Service	Level 1	Level 2	Level 3	Level 4	Total
The reception,					
including food					
Wedding cake					
Beverages					
Gratuities for the					
bartenders and waiters					
Decorations					
Music: Organist/Pianist					
Soloist/Choir					
Reception Music					
Flowers					
A special wedding gift					
for the newlyweds					
The bride's wedding					
attire and trousseau					
Invitations					
Announcements					
Mailing costs					
Photography and					
videography:					
Engagement photos					
Wedding photographs					
Video of the wedding					
Video of the reception					
Rental of sanctuary or					
other marriage site					
Aisle carpets					

Canopies and tents_____

Additional costs for

 decorations_____

Bridesmaids' bouquets_____

Gratuities to those

   directing traffic_____

Parking costs and

 valets_____

Transportation for

 bridal party to the

 wedding ceremony and

 from ceremony to reception_____

The bridesmaids'

 luncheon_____

The Groom's Family's Traditional Responsibilities

Service	Level 1	Level 2	Level 3	Level 4	Total
Father of the groom's clothes for the wedding					
Travel expenses and hotel bills his family may incur					
A wedding gift for bride and groom					
The rehearsal dinner					

Creating A Vendor List

A comprehensive vendor list is one of the best resources a wedding consultant can possess. You need to meet with these vendors and ask them for price ranges of three levels of service each one of them provides. As you work with vendors, ask them to supply photos of their products. You will need photos that are representative of products at each of the three different prices levels so you can clearly illustrate the differences to your clients.

Many of the businesses that support weddings are not well trained in marketing, so it is to your advantage to think like a marketer for them. Florists and other vendors may be reluctant at first to openly share their range of prices with you. In order to overcome this, you need to help them understand what an advantage it will be to them if you are selling their services to your clients. When you do this, not only will they share their prices, but they will work extra hard to help you become successful in every wedding. Show them the Wedding Cost Worksheet you will be using and ask them where they want to fit into that profile.

Some vendors will naturally fall into level one, and others in levels two or three. When you find a vendor you really like, encourage them to offer their services or products at each of the three different price levels. This will increase the probability that your client will choose their service. It is important to let each vendor know that you will show clients a chart of comparisons, and that you will describe the benefits of each, but the actual choice rests with the client.

The following worksheet is a Vendor List Worksheet for your personal use only. This is a helpful way for you to keep track of vendors' services and their prices. You need to keep this list as up-to-date as possible, because this will be your source document when you prepare the Wedding Cost Worksheet that you will provide to your clients. This is a personal worksheet, while the Wedding Cost Worksheet is the "marketing" tool you will use with your clients.

As you talk to vendors, ask them to keep you informed about any price changes they make. This will help you keep your prices current, but don't rely on them entirely to do this for you. Some will not be that organized or they may forget. Because of this you will need to personally contact any vendor you haven't used in the past thirty days to make sure you have their latest prices before you prepare the Wedding Cost Worksheet for a couple with whom you are working.

MoneyMaker Tip: Since you are building your own marketing pieces, and making worksheets, you may want to charge vendors for your assistance. If you have a natural talent for building marketing pieces, why not sell that service to your vendors?

VENDOR LIST WORKSHEET

Vendor Information	Level 1	Level 2	Level 3	Level 4

Bakeries

> *[insert vendor name]*
>
> *[address]*
>
> *[phone]*
>
> *[insert name of key contact]*

Balloons

> *[insert vendor name]*
>
> *[address]*
>
> *[phone]*
>
> *[insert name of key contact]*

Cake Tops

> *[insert vendor name]*
>
> *[address]*
>
> *[phone]*
>
> *[insert name of key contact]*

Ceremony Locations (Include parks, churches, synagogues, and local chapels)

> *[insert vendor name]*
>
> *[address]*
>
> *[phone]*
>
> *[insert name of key contact]*

Clergy/ Wedding Officiants

> *[insert vendor name]*
>
> *[address]*
>
> *[phone]*
>
> *[insert name of key contact]*

Florists

> *[insert vendor name]*

[address]

[phone]

[insert name of key contact]

Printers/ Stationery

[insert vendor name]

[address]

[phone]

[insert name of key contact]

Make-up/Hair

[insert vendor name]

[address]

[phone]

[insert name of key contact]

Music

[insert vendor name]

[address]

[phone]

[insert name of key contact]

Rentals

[insert vendor name]

[address]

[phone]

[insert name of key contact]

Photographers

[insert vendor name]

[address]

[phone]

[insert name of key contact]

Reception Halls

[insert vendor name]

[address]

[phone]

[insert name of key contact]

Registries

[insert vendor name]

[address]

[phone]

[insert name of key contact]

Transportation

[insert vendor name]

[address]

[phone]

[insert name of key contact]

Tuxedos

[insert vendor name]

[address]

[phone]

[insert name of key contact]

Video

[insert vendor name]

[address]

[phone]

[insert name of key contact]

A good rule of thumb is to have a minimum of two vendors in each category. You cannot adequately provide the services you desire with fewer than two. In many categories, you should aim at four or five vendors. This list will obviously grow as your business grows.

One of the best things you can do to build your business is to use this list as your appointment schedule. Make it a practice to contact a minimum of three vendors a week, and before long you will not only have a valuable list of vendors, some of those vendors will recommend your services to their customers.

Be Flexible With Different Ideas

There is no such thing as a typical wedding anymore. The trends of the '90s certainly have changed people's ideas about what they want their weddings to be. Although some weddings these days will be quite extravagant, many weddings are still small. A wedding can be a simple, low-key backyard ceremony, or it can be a lavish affair, complete with extraordinary accents and held in a stunningly romantic setting. Most likely, a wedding today is something between these two extremes.

Ultimately the size and extravagance of the wedding will be determined by the couple's (and their families') budgets and by their preferences. With costs for wedding services being so high, many couples will choose to manage the cost of having a grand wedding by limiting the number of guests. Others may choose to limit the number of wedding attendants while they splurge on the reception. It's up to you as a consultant to listen carefully to the bride and groom to make sure you understand what they want. Sometimes they will not be quite sure what they want and your job will be to help them decide.

Keep in mind that it is not your job to influence them strongly to do one thing or another. Your job is to present options and information so they can make informed decisions. In the end it is your job to take whatever plans the bride and groom decide upon and carry out these plans, regardless of the wedding size.

Nationally, the average cost of a formal wedding with 188 guests is $17,470, according to Modern Bride Magazine. This figure does not include the cost of a honeymoon, which can add several thousand dollars to wedding costs.

Obviously costs vary in direct relation to the size and scope of the wedding the couple chooses. This is an area where your services can be very valuable to the couple. Offering advice is one of the major duties of a consultant. The more you know and understand about wedding practices and vendor's services, the more you will be able to build an excellent business reputation. As you work with the couple, show them alternatives that will make their wedding day extra special, no matter how much or how little they have to spend.

You also need to be aware of your own skills in managing a wedding. It's important that you not take on a larger wedding than you are comfortable handling alone. If when you work with a couple, it becomes very clear to you that they are planning a much larger affair than you are comfortable handling, you may want to collaborate with another consultant, even though you will have to give up some of your income. It is easiest to feel good about this when you understand these things: when you give up some of your income, you are in effect making an investment in your own knowledge. Next time you will be more comfortable with a wedding of this magnitude or even larger. Secondly you will ensure that this wedding takes place without a hitch, thereby making sure that your reputation grows as someone who can handle large, expensive weddings.

The key is to do something both you and they are comfortable with. If you try to do something that's over what they can spend or exceeds your capacity, it can turn into a real headache. It's important to keep things in perspective. Setting priorities is the key to planning and budgeting a wedding.

The consultant has to help the bridal couple determine what is important to them and what they want their guests to remember when they leave the wedding. Whether it's the food, the band, or the setting-whatever they decide is most important, the consultant can not skimp on that. And, it doesn't depend only on their budget. Attention to detail is often what makes a wedding special. One way to help a couple develop priorities and make decisions is to have them work through the Wedding Planning Priority Worksheet that follows:

Directions:

Step One: Make a list of all the things the bride and groom desire. Follow the rules of brainstorming by encouraging them to make a complete list of their "dream" wedding. Encourage them not to rate or evaluate the ideas, just make a list.

Step Two: Write their ideas in any order Wedding Planning Priority Worksheet. If they have more than twelve ideas, expand the chart.

Step Three: Begin the process of identifying which ideas are more important by comparing each line with the others on the page, one at a time. The numbers on the right are used to narrow the list by making comparisons of each item with each other item on the list. For example, at the end of line 2 are the numbers 1 and 2. If they think item one is more important than item two, then circle the number 1. Circle 2 if they think item two is more important to them. Next move to line three. The first pair of numbers is 1 and 3. Compare item one with item three; circle the number of the more important item. The next pair of numbers is 2 and 3. Compare item two with item three, again circling the number of the more important item. Continue doing this down this list. You will compare every item on the list with every item above it on the list. Circle the number in the pair of numbers that represent the more important of the two items they are comparing. Continue the process until all twelve have been compared.

Step Four: Count up the number of times you circled each number and write that on the line to the far left of the numbers. For example, count every time you circled the number 1 on the list. If you circled the number 1 six times, write the number six beside item one on the list. As you continue to do this for every item on the list, you and the couple will discover their real preferences among all the items on the list.

WEDDING PLANNING PRIORITY WORKSHEET

What are we planning? _____

_____   1.   _____

_____   2.   _____   1
                                              2

_____   3.   _____   1   2
                                              3   3

_____   4.   _____   1   2   3
                                              4   4   4

_____   5.   _____   1   2   3   4
                                              5   5   5   5

_____   6.   _____   1   2   3   4   5
                                              6   6   6   6   6

_____   7.   _____   1   2   3   4   5   6
                                              7   7   7   7   7   7

_____   8.   _____   1   2   3   4   5   6   7
                                              8   8   8   8   8   8   8

_____   9.   _____   1   2   3   4   5   6   7   8
                                              9   9   9   9   9   9   9   9

_____   10.   _____   1   2   3   4   5   6   7   8   9
                                             10   10   10   10   10   10   10   10   10

_____   11.   _____   1   2   3   4   5   6   7   8   9   10
                                             11   11   11   11   11   11   11   11   11   11

_____   12.   _____   1   2   3   4   5   6   7   8   9   10   11
                                             12   12   12   12   12   12   12   12   12   12   12

List the top five priorities ...

1. _____

2. _____

3. _____

4. _____

5. _____

Some General Costs Information

The following is a sampling of activities and nation-wide average costs involved with the major elements of a formal wedding. These costs will vary from one community to another, but they can be used as a benchmark for your own learning. Please keep in mind that these are merely suggestions.

Catering

Caterers are usually the largest expense and can cost more than half of the entire cost of the wedding. Tastes run from caviar to chicken, so there is a wide range of catering costs. The general trend in wedding catering is toward healthy foods and combined cuisines, such as American combined with French. Serving stations are also becoming more popular because of people's diverse tastes.

Where the couple chooses to hold their wedding and the type of food they want to have served will determine the choice of caterers. Intimate winery or garden settings for weddings are gaining in popularity and may be just as elegant as those held in a sanctuary. The garden weddings lend themselves to what are called food stations, rather than a buffet or sit-down dinner. Four or five different food stations provide a more casual and relaxed feel for the reception. Different ethnic foods such as a pasta bar, oriental appetizers, German food, Mexican food can be served at separate stations. Dessert bars can be set up as well in addition to the food stations.

Also don't forget a coffee bar, featuring not only standard regular and decaffeinated coffees, but lattes, cappuccinos, or flavored coffees. The extent of the coffee bar should be in direct correlation to the "fanciness" of the dessert bar. Again, it is up to you as consultant to suggest and for the couple to decide.

In the lower range of catering prices you can expect the cost to range between $25 and $50 per person. These typically include non-butlered appetizers and a chicken entree, with a beer, wine, and soda bar.

In the middle range are catering packages that cost between $50 and $75 per person. These may include light appetizers, a beef carving station, or a chicken or fish entree, with an open bar featuring non-premium brands.

For a gourmet feast consisting of a five-course meal with a premium open bar, the bridal couple can pay up to $100 per person. This would include seafood hors d'oeuvres served by butlers, a premium entree such as filet mignon, lobster, veal, salmon or lamb, and creative side dishes such as asparagus in raspberry vinaigrette dressing or wild mushroom polenta.

Two issues that are related to catering but may be provided by different vendors are the wedding cake and the rehearsal meal. Let's look at these two services quickly beginning with the wedding cake.

The wedding cake is frequently provided by a bakery and not by the caterer. Sometimes you may get a much better price, however, if it is provided by the caterer and factored into the catering price. Wedding cake prices can range from $2.25 to $5.95 per slice.

The rehearsal dinner is the other item that may be factored into the catering price, although it usually is not done. Casual rehearsal dinners are a current trend that you need to be aware of. Rehearsal dinners may be as casual as a barbecue, pizza party or a picnic. As the consultant, bring up these ideas with your clients. Many times, simple inexpensive ideas such as these do not occur to the couple.

Reception Costs

Another major expense of weddings and probably the second largest expense after catering are the wedding reception and its site. The wedding may include such reception locations as museums and grand estates. Sometimes the reception site also provides in-house catering as a package deal. This arrangement is common among restaurants, hotels, and country clubs.

Basic rental charges for reception sites have an extremely wide range. Renting a union hall, an auditorium or a museum building, for example, can cost as little as $250 and run up to about $400.

MoneyMaker Tip: Look for unique but affordable settings in your community. Many can be reserved for little or no cost. You may be able to generate a whole new business opportunity turning different sites into marriage sites. A few wedding consultants have segmented their services by specializing in unique or novel weddings.

In the middle price range, a stately mansion or historic building can provide an elegant site for a wedding party. These range in price from $800 to $1,500.

At the upper end are unique and unforgettable sites. These can range in cost from $1,500 and $2,000 and beyond. These include local mansions with spectacular architecture, with tiers and pillars and wrought iron balconies and marble floors.

Flowers

Flowers are more than fragrant accessories. Brides are choosing bouquets based on the special meaning each flower has. There are few set rules regarding flowers anymore. Wedding flowers have a broad price range depending on the bridal couple's preferences.

In the lower price range, some floral wedding packages start as low as $80. This includes bouquets and boutonnieres of carnations, daisies and baby's breath.

In the middle price range, some florists offer flower packages that range from $700 to $3,000. The higher end of this price range would include centerpieces for the tables in addition to flowers for the church pews and aisles, and the reception.

In the upper price range, flower packages start at around $3,000 for 200 seated guests and may range upwards of $15,000. The arrangements include a wide variety of roses and lilies, as well as more unusual flowers.

Photography

Wedding photography has changed drastically over the years. It is very important that you as consultant stay up on the various trends. Despite all of the advances in color film processing, black and white prints are enjoying a comeback among couples who are seeking a more classic, timeless look to their wedding photography.

What is surprising is that black and white photography actually costs more than color because the technology of black and white photography has simply not kept pace with color, and as such, added costs are common. Don't be caught off guard thinking black and white will save money.

Couples often choose to have about 20 percent of their wedding prints done in black and white, and then either intersperse them with the color prints in the album or separate them.

Another aspect of wedding photography is video. You may have clients consider recording the printed photographic proofs of their wedding recorded on video. It is much less expensive to duplicate video than to duplicate the printed proofs. The duplicated videos can then be mailed to friends and relatives who want to select photos from the proofs. In addition, the proofs can then be chosen simultaneously and the album can be completed much sooner.

You might want to suggest that the couple think about having disposable cameras on each table for guests to use and leave behind. The benefit of this technique is that the couple sees the wedding from the perspective of the guests.

When the pictures are developed, the couple can include a photo of each guest in the thank you notes. This makes a very nice and sensitive personal touch that allows your guest to feel like more than just a face in the crowd.

Due to the high cost of photography and videography, a good wedding consultant will have several vendors in mind, ones who perform a variety of tasks. Basic wedding photography packages usually involve about seven to eight hours of shooting time and include a bridal photo album with several dozen prints. A basic wedding package starts around $1,500 and includes about 30 - 8x10 prints and one - 11x14 portrait. The number of albums, prints and enlargements can raise the price to about $2,500.

To save money on photography, sometimes the consultant can arrange a package deal with the reception site or caterer to have photography included in those costs. But, quality does vary widely, and some large photography houses have assistants or understudies who do the actual shooting in these cases.

Travel and Entertainment

As for transportation, a six-passenger limousine, black or white, rents for about $180 for three hours. Typically, a limousine will carry the bridal party from the bride's home to the ceremony, and afterward take the bride and groom to the reception. Do not sit ring bearers or flower girls near the bride in the limousine. It is easy for their feet to get on the bride's dress or some other tragedy to occur, such as being sick during the ride.

Musical entertainment is another area where decisions can be difficult. Does your couple want their guests to swing to the sounds of big band music or leap to the pounding rhythms of new wave rock? Whatever their musical taste, there is a band, classical ensemble or disc jockey who can suit your needs. Bands are more expensive, ranging up to $3,500, but they add a special touch and an elegant musical accompaniment to the event.

Disc jockeys start as low as $200 for four hours and can range up to $600, depending on the time involved and the type of equipment used. Some disc jockeys use broadcast-quality sound equipment and can also supply a light show or karaoke equipment. This usually runs about $325 for four hours. Most karaoke disc jockeys will have a library of everything from classic lounge hits to country to rock.

Gowns and Tuxedos

The bride's gown is another area in which the consultant can provide much needed assistance. The consultant must be aware of where to find the most attractive gown at the lowest price. The bride will, of course, decide on the style, but you as the consultant can steer her in the right direction for the price. At the bottom of the price spectrum, the bride can go to a department store and buy a gown off the rack for a few hundred dollars.

For more selection, she can go to a bridal wear shop, where the average wedding gown costs about $800. At the higher end of the price spectrum are places where the average gown sells for about $1,500 and prices go up to about $4,000 for top-of-the-line designer gowns.

For the groom, there are rental tuxedos widely available in the $30 to $80 price range, or he can buy a tuxedo starting at about $300 and going up to $800 for a top-notch Christian Dior.

Miscellaneous

Other miscellaneous costs, on the average, are:

✔ videographer, about $450;

✔ invitations/announcements, about $350;

✔ fees for clergy, about $200 (depending on the formality and extent of the service);

✔ headpiece/veil, about $175;

✔ attendants' attire for five, about $750; and

✔ men's formal-wear rentals for five, about $550.

One area in which you should make suggestions concerns what the guests can toss at the wedding couple following the reception as they leave for their honeymoon. Birdseed and rice are no longer acceptable for a variety of reasons. But, there are many alternatives. One idea is to release butterflies into the air around the couple. Another is to toss rose petals at them. A favorite that is coming into play at many outdoor weddings is that the guests are each given a small bottle of bubble solution and a wand. As the bride and groom kiss, each guest dips a wand into the bottle and blows dozens of bubbles. The bride and groom see bubbles, like good wishes, soaring upward. Make sure the photographer and videographer capture this on print and video. The effect is gorgeous.

Keep in mind that a wedding coordinator or consultant is not just for the wealthy anymore. A professional saves time, money and provides expert assistance, whether the wedding affair is extravagant or "down home simple." Your knowledge of each aspect of the wedding can enhance everyone's wedding and provide you with a very good income.

CHAPTER EIGHT

DEALING WITH VENDORS

Finding the Best Vendors

New brides want a smooth trip down the aisle without having to worry about all the little, yet numerous details that help this come to pass. This transition from single lady to married woman can be uncomplicated by you, the wedding coordinator. It is up to you to handle every detail that stands in the way of making this bride's wishes come true.

As this book has mentioned time and again, the budget is the starting point for all these decisions. Only by following this budget to the nickel can these needs be successfully met. The first time you provide a service, you may have to shop around for the best and most trusted vendors, but over time you will become well acquainted with all the vendors in your community.

It is time to discuss each of the vendors that you as the consultant may be recommending. One of the most important things you can do for your couples is to become well-acquainted with each of the vendors in community. If you live in a small town, you may even need to know vendors in the surrounding geographic area. If you don't recommend and use reliable, professional vendors, their bad reputation will reflect on your businesses. So once again, make sure you know the vendors you recommend.

One of the best ways to come to know your vendors is to complete a Vendor Survey on each one. This survey can either be mailed out, or completed during a visit to their offices.

VENDOR SURVEY

1. Vendor Information

Name of the Business: _____

Address: _____

_____

Phone: (   ) __ __ __ - __ __ __ __

Fax: (   ) __ __ __ - __ __ __ __

Email:

2. Key Personnel:

Owner: _____   Staff: _____

Staff: _____   Staff: _____

3. Business History/References

How long have you been in business?

Can you provide two former customers as references?

_____   _____
Name   Phone

_____   _____
Name   Phone

4. Services

What wedding services do you provide?

What experience do you have working with consultants?

5. What other consulting relationships do you have. Please list their names below:

It is a good idea for you to check out each vendor with the Better Business Bureau and the Chamber of Commerce for your city. Look for complaints as well as compliments on the companies you are considering. Do not be afraid of asking questions. Your reputation as a fine consultant depends on their reliability and quality of service.

As you visit vendors, notice the quality of their equipment and delivery vehicles. Do they present the type of image you want to associate with? How do they relate to their clients? Are they friendly? How do they speak about their customers? Ask if you can attend a wedding they are serving to get a better feel for the work they do.

MoneyMaker Tip: Although it is not ideal, in the beginning, you may be able to contract your time to these vendors and work as their assistant. You learn their business in depth and can pay the bills until your business takes off. Often these relationships lead to many years of successful partnering.

During the visit, some will be very comfortable talking about their business practices and are quite willing to help a newcomer out. When you find this person, begin building a good relationship. You also want to know what day(s) they take off, and what their business hours are, because many weddings run into the late night hours or occur on Saturday.

Shopping for Services

Most bridal shops and major department stores will give you information about reliable vendors. Take time to sample their foods, view floral arrangements, and check out the bridal salons, tuxedo rental stores and other clothing shops in your area. You want a ready list of proven and trustworthy recommendations of vendors for every single aspect of any wedding you are asked to coordinate. Don't wait until you are asked for a recommendation and have to tell the bride you will check it out. Plan to study everyone as one of the first things you do as you open your consulting business. By doing your homework ahead of time, you will gain the confidence of your wedding couple that you know your profession well.

As you get acquainted with each vendor, it is important to discuss contracts. Your position in discussing contracts needs to be that you work on a basis of binding contracts, with no excuses allowed for breaking the contract. You need to be sure that every business, from jewelry stores to wedding cakes, will sign a contract that they will live up to. Without a contract, there is no guarantee that you will get what you ask for or that the vendor will even show up!

When you make a contract with a vendor, you should specify both the product and accompanying services that the vendor is expected to provide. Make sure the contract states the dates the service is to be performed, the times they are to be on site and if appropriate, the name brands of the products that you prefer. You should also include in the contract how billing for their services will be handled and paid (which will be discussed shortly). This should include cancellation and refund policies and charges for overtime, if any. It would be an excellent idea for you to make a contract checklist before you making any contractual agreements, just to make sure you don't omit anything important from the contract.

Read the contract over thoroughly several times to be sure that you do not leave out or miss any important item. If, by some chance, you need to change something in the contract, do it in writing or use certified mail. Registered mail is even better since the recipient must return a postcard stating that the individual specified on the letter actually received it. That gives you absolute proof that they received a copy of your revisions. But written proof should never be the only way you deal with your vendors. You also need to confirm change either face-to-face or by telephone as well. This way you can discuss any issues that may arise because of the change in the contract.

The bridal party will have numerous questions as they are deciding upon vendors. And that's good. In the following sections we will go over most of the questions the bride and groom are likely to ask when you are working with them to plan their wedding.

The Wedding Gown

When it comes to wedding attire and accessories most questions will generally relate to traditional weddings, but whatever kind of wedding the couple wants, the questions are generally the same.

Finding the perfect wedding gown is one of the most important questions pressing on the bride's mind. Searching for the right one can be both challenging and pleasurable. Many times the consultant will accompany the bride and her mother on their search for just the right one. Since the consultant has done her homework and knows which places have the gowns that match the bride's expectations and budget, she can lead the bride in the right direction.

Wedding gowns come in many styles, fabrics, and price ranges. Gowns vary from simple informal ones to elaborate, elegant gowns with intricate beading and trains of various lengths. The choice of fabrics used in the gown can greatly affect the cost of the gown. Keep the following thoughts in mind as the bride searches for her ideal gown.

Help the bride get some idea of what she is looking for long before she begins to actually shop. Make sure you have lots of bridal magazines to choose from. One hint is that you can keep magazines and advertisements from you favorite vendors in plain sight for your client to become interested in.

You may want to buy a three-inch three-ring binder and a set of index tabs to organize your bridal gown book. Clip pictures of all styles of wedding gowns from bridal magazines, insert them in clear three-ring sheet protectors. Be sure to separate them by various styles.

On your index tabs, label them informal, formal, street length, short trains, long trains, etc. The idea is to group them in similar styles behind each tab. This saves the bride a great deal of time and hassle. It helps the bride clearly see what she wants and it makes it easy to communicate with the people where the gown is being purchased, exactly what the bride prefers.

Although the exact gown pictured in your binder may not be the one she buys, it may be one very similar. Your "look-through" binder will be an excellent tool for a bride who has a mental picture of her ideal gown, but can't quite describe it in words.

Sometimes the bride will bring you a picture that she has cut from a bridal magazine of the exact gown she wants. This does not happen often, but you need to be prepared in case it does. Tell her you will take the clipping to a bridal shop and see if they can order it. The bridal shop can then contact you as to whether they can order the gown, how long it will take to get it, and how much it will cost.

Be sure to report back to the bride, giving her all the particulars, and obtaining her authorization before you have the bridal shop place the order. If one bridal shop cannot order the preferred gown, then go to another one (depending on the reason why the first one could not). All of this means you have a bride who knows what she wants and it is to your advantage to serve her well.

Keep in mind it never hurts to push the vendors from whom you can make the most money, as long as they are perfectly professional and totally reliable.

MoneyMaker Tip: Although it is a minor point, magazines are now a business expense and tax deductible. Imagine, now you can buy all the magazines you want and deduct the expense from your business taxes. These magazines provoke thought and stimulate creativity.

Keep in mind that wedding gowns are personal and should be chosen based on the bride's individual style preference, the type of wedding, the location of the wedding, and her budget. Almost anything is acceptable, so let the final decision be hers, unless she is going over her budget.

Bridal gowns can be purchased or ordered from a variety of places. Bridal salons, discount warehouses and outlets, resale and consignment shops, and custom designers are some places to consider. As the consultant, it is your obligation to consult with these places long before the bride arrives. You should have full knowledge of what they offer, the low and high price ranges, the services that go with it (such as altering, cleaning, etc.), their hours, and anything else that might pertain to helping brides find their perfect dress from the perfect vendor.

Many of the boutique bridal shops require an appointment or have limited hours. These shops are generally more expensive than others. Their sales force is very knowledgeable of their gowns and carry accessories such as gloves, jewelry, and shoes that coordinate or complement their gowns.

Most of the other bridal stores also have salespeople who know their product and can assist the bride with selecting the right gown. If the gown is new and to be ordered, she must allow at least four months for fittings, manufacture and delivery. Advise the bride that she must allow extra time to guard against the possibility of something going wrong. For example, there could be a delay in delivery of the gown, they could send the wrong gown altogether, or the gown could possibly be damaged in transit. In your consultation with the bride at the beginning stages, make sure that you discuss these time elements with her.

You must be sure that the companies you recommend are not "fly-by-night" outfits. It is not difficult to imagine the chaos that would result if, on the day of the delivery of the gown, you discover that the person or firm with whom you are dealing is no longer in business. It is up to you to keep tabs on the progress of the gown. The best protection is to deal with a firm that has long been established in the community, a store that has a national affiliation, or a shop that has qualified as an authorized dealer or representative for a nationally recognized product name.

Manufactured wedding gowns make the need for reliability of the vendor even more important because a non-refundable deposit is almost always required at the time the gown is ordered. A quality bridal gown vendor will also be able to assist the bride or consultant if problems are encountered in the manufacture or delivery process.

You should never let yourself be intimidated by the salesperson who is assisting you and the bride. Since you are in the process of soliciting reputable vendors, you need to almost be on the offensive. Most vendors understand the importance of offering quality service and quality products. Therefore, feel free to ask questions about anything you are unsure of. Be sure to satisfy yourself that there are no additional or hidden costs, such as for steaming or final alterations. If you are satisfied it is more likely that your client will also be satisfied.

As with all the vendors you use in your business, no matter how well you know them or how often you have used their services, always insist that all of the essential terms of your agreement with the salesperson be in writing. Do not proceed on the basis of an oral agreement or understanding. Unfortunately, should you and the salesperson later disagree on the terms of your agreement, the salesperson will have a distinct advantage in the negotiation process if you do not get that written agreement.

There's one other eventuality you need to prepare for concerning wedding gowns. Sometimes a bride may want to wear the gown her grandmother or mother wore at her wedding, but it does not fit. It is important for you to know of seamstresses who specialize in altering fine garments such as wedding gowns. Once again, it's extremely important to do your homework in advance of this event. Nothing could be more disastrous than having a seamstress you are not sure of permanently ruining an heirloom wedding gown. It could even be disastrous to your own income.

How Formal Should They Go?

There are no hard and fast rules so far as wedding attire is concerned. The outfitting of your client's wedding should be determined totally by her personal preferences, taking into consideration her budget. But you can assist the bride with her decision by explaining the differences in formal wear, semiformal wear and informal wear. These types would be determined by the time of day that the wedding would be held, as well.

A formal wedding can be held at any time of the day, but is particularly appropriate if the ceremony and reception are planned for the evening. The bride is ordinarily attired in a full-length gown and the groom in black or white tuxedo. The bridesmaids' dresses and the groomsmen's suits should complement the attire worn by the bride and groom.

A semiformal wedding is, as the title implies, less traditional than a formal ceremony. The bride's gown may be of any length desired. The groom and his groomsmen may wear suits or black tuxedos. The formality of the clothing worn by the bridesmaids and groomsmen may be toned down accordingly.

An informal wedding offers maximum flexibility. The bride ordinarily will wear either a traditional gown or a tailored suit. A suit is appropriate for the groom.

In the final analysis, the decision regarding the wedding attire is entirely the bride's and groom's. Let them know that they need not feel bound to follow the rules set down by others. It is, after all, their wedding day.

Wedding Rings

The purchase of the wedding jewelry should be an exciting part of your business. Unfortunately, in today's marketplace, jewelry shopping can often be a confusing experience. This is where you, as the consultant, come in. You know already that you need to be well acquainted with all the jewelry vendors in the area. You need to research all of them and know where to obtain the best services at the best prices. Since there is so much competition in this field, you can expect to receive conflicting information, most of it intended to sell you rather than assist you. Here are some basic tips that can help you cut through the technical jargon and sales tactics.

Your first stops should be locally owned jewelry stores that have established a good reputation over a number of years. It's also a good idea to look for a store with an in-house jeweler so any sizing or custom work can be performed on the premises. A jeweler who is rooted in the community has a vested interest in making you a satisfied customer because they typically advertise by "word-of-mouth," just as you do.

In recommending a shop for purchasing the wedding rings, most consumers have difficulty choosing a wedding ring because of the many variables involved in diamond quality and value. Diamond grading is broken down into "Four C's": carat, clarity, color and cut. All of these add up to a "Fifth C": cost. Ask how the "Four C's" apply to the ring or rings that they are considering. Often if this is a vendor that you frequently recommend and one that your clients regularly purchase from, you may be able to get a better price than others might.

Before the bride and groom reach a final decision on their rings, there are several other considerations they should take into account. The first one is the matter of how long it will take to have the ring sized. If the ring is being ordered from an outside jeweler or manufacturer, how much time will be required for delivery and size adjustments, if necessary? Allowance of sufficient time in advance of the wedding date is essential.

As with all prospective vendors, ask lots of questions. Good salespeople like to share their knowledge and experience. Visit a number of jewelry outlets. Take good notes and compare them as you study what they offer. When you give this information to the bride-to-be, make sure you also offer them this advice: don't make snap decisions. Think about it overnight. Tell them which vendor's financing terms are competitive. Trust yourself and your own eye. If something doesn't look right, it probably isn't. The bride and groom need to make the choice that is right for them, not what someone else wants to sell them. Encourage them not to rush and to enjoy this special occasion. This will allow the bridal couple to choose what they want with care. Keep in mind this is a decision that will probably last them the rest of their lives.

Bridal Registry

Regardless of the type of wedding you're planning, the age of the couple or their budget, their friends and family want to give them a wedding gift. They want to give something they need and want. You know yourself how good it feels to give someone a gift they really like. Everyone likes to believe his gift is special and won't be returned after the wedding. Bridal registries are a service for their family and friends as well as for the bridal couple themselves.

This is a very important subject that you need to be well prepared for. If you develop a personalized bridal registry list, it will help your clients get a good start on the creation of their new life together. After the stress and rushing around of the wedding, reception and honeymoon, it's great to come home to the things that will make them comfortable and relaxed. With the proper bridal registry information, you'll have happy clients and the couple will have many of the necessities for their new home.

Today's bridal registries are putting a new spin on tradition. Sure, the couple may register for china, silver, and crystal, but they will also register for sheets, towels, cookware, bakeware, cutlery, and appliances. These are the things they need for everyday living. Their friends will want to know their favorite colors, the size of their bed, what pieces of cookware they need, and if they already have certain appliances. By registering, they'll get one toaster, not five!

An experienced, professional bridal registry consultant has the product knowledge to help them with their selections. It can be a little overwhelming when there are so many decisions, so many details, and so little time to take care of everything. It's important that you, as the consultant, have confidence in all of your registry consultants so that you can pass this confidence on to the bride.

Advise your bride to register about five to eight months before the wedding. This assures that her list will be in place before any parties or showers. Most companies will maintain the registry for at least one year after the wedding date. When researching companies for your client's wish list, there are several things to consider. First is customer service. You'll want the guests to be treated well, and you'll want it to be a positive experience if it is necessary to make exchanges after the wedding.

Next is accessibility. Will it be easy for your bride's guests to obtain her list and the items on it? Selection, quality, and prices are important, too. Giving accurate and price-conscious advice to your bridal couple will make all the difference in their successful household set-up.

Make an appointment with the bridal registry consultant to discuss their particular registry. Get to know the people involved and their line of products. Then, inform the bride of what she should expect when she sees the bridal registry consultant. The bride should make an appointment with the consultant. The registry consultant should set aside an hour to an hour and a half for your client. Suggest to her that it's best to go in a day or two before her appointment to look around. That way, she will have an idea of the things she might want on her list, and won't be overwhelmed by all of the questions she will have to answer.

Your job, as the bride's consultant, is to be sure that each registry consultant at each store on your vendor list is expertly knowledgeable on what their particular store offers and has a complete, comfortable list of questions to ask the prospective bride. Bridal registry is a complementary service. The time with a registry consultant and the servicing of the bride's list is free. What her friends and relatives choose for her will be profit for their store. It will be the easiest part of her wedding plans, and the most profitable for her.

Remember to choose someone you and the bride have confidence in and have fun developing her wish list. Also, make sure the bride considers the possibility that some people who never shop at upscale department stores may feel a registry at this store is pretentious and too expensive for their wallet. Make sure you have a list of alternative stores available for the bride to choose. An increasing number of types of stores are offering registry services, including hardware stores. If she registers at a wide selection of store types she will serve her guests, friends and family well. A well-orchestrated registry should make life a lot easier for everyone. Your client will appreciate the time you spent finding the best registries for her needs, and her guests will appreciate the time the bride spent making their gift selection so easy and convenient.

Wedding and Reception Sites

Two of the most important areas that a bridal consultant involves herself in are the locations for the wedding and reception for clients. These are the places that will be remembered forever. Keep in mind that the reception and caterers generally wind up being the most costly area of the wedding.

As you visit possible wedding and/or reception sites, keep notes of your observations and the information you obtain. Ask whether the quoted price is all inclusive, or whether there will be additional charges, such as gratuities, overtime fees, and sales tax. Insist that all details be in writing, including dates, times, prices, and description of services provided. Ask about the payment requirements. Most sites will require a down payment to reserve the facility, with the balance due approximately one week prior to the date of the event, when the final guest count is known.

Nowadays, weddings and receptions are not only held in churches. They can be held just about anywhere. Some of these will be discussed in an upcoming chapter, but it is important to remember that Saturday night is the most expensive time to schedule weddings and receptions. To save money, advise the bridal couple to consider another evening or a weekend afternoon. Morning or afternoon weddings also call for a lighter menu, so they may be able to save on the catering as well.

Flowers

As you shop around for the vendors you will recommend to your bride and groom, florists are nearly at the top of the list. Finding reputable, professional florists can be tricky. Most shops have lovely arrangements adorning their windows and even the shelves inside the shops. But it's important for you to know what they can provide for the weddings your clients choose. Can they deliver the goods that are paid for? Can they provide the specific flowers requested? Are the flowers they provide always fresh? What happens if the plans change?

Weddings are costly, and everyone is interested in saving money if possible. Floral designs created from fresh and silk flowers may help your couple stay within their budget. Whether or not your vendor can and will supply silk rather than arranged real flowers is another question to ask.

As a wedding consultant, you need to have a variety of floral vendors for your couple to choose from. Therefore, as you look around, remember to check for all kinds of services the vendor can offer. Keep in mind that some florists are more creative than others are. As usual, ask questions. Can the bride choose wedding flowers that either can serve more than one function or can be kept as a remembrance of the occasion? Ask them to show you samples of all their different arrangements. How do they make wedding arrangements? Are wedding arrangement a normal source of their business? If not, you should continue looking for vendors who do the majority of business with weddings. You may want to start a floral arrangement photo booklet to help the bride make better decisions about the size and style of the arrangements.

There are several types of arrangements needed for weddings. Make sure that the florists provide the following types of arrangements:

✔ Standing baskets filled with sprays of fresh or silk flowers. These provide decoration for the ceremony and can later be moved to the reception site, where they look elegant placed behind the head table or at the entrance to the room.

✔ Decorations for arches. Be sure to ask whether the florist provides these and how they are done. An arch is useful at the site of the ceremony, in a garden wedding, or the bride may wish to make her entrance under a flower covered arch before being escorted down the aisle. If the arch is made of silk flowers, the newlyweds can retain this. It's a great item for bringing back fond memories of the wedding day.

✔ Swags or floral centerpieces for the head table. If these are made of permanent live plants they can be a lovely addition to a first home.

It is a good idea to decide who will inherit the flowers after the reception. Live plants can become part of the bride and groom's new home, but if the couple has decided to invest a great deal of money in floral decorations, they may have more than they can handle in their new home. In any event, they should not go to waste. They may want to remember "special friends" by assigning floral arrangements to them. One other option, when there are "too many" flowers is to have someone deliver arrangements to a local nursing home where they would be greatly appreciated.

In addition to flowers for the bride and the wedding and reception sites, the florist must be able to outfit the attendants and flower girls. The attendants' flowers will parallel those of the bride. The florist typically makes a smaller simpler arrangement for the flower girl. One additional nice touch would be a simple silk wreath made of ribbon, tulle and tiny flowers made up for the bride. This can be enjoyed after the wedding day hung on a wall, on the brim of a straw hat or displayed in the home.

Again, a contract is essential when dealing with floral vendors. There are a few important questions that you must ask each of them as you seek out the best. What are their regular fees? How do they charge? Are there fees for "special requests?" How are they rated? Are there additional fees for arrangement set-up? Are there fees for breakage? What about hidden fees? These are just a few of the questions you should ask prospective florists. The wants and the needs of the bride and groom must be clearly set out in the contract. Then if the florist fails at delivering in conjunction with the bride's plans, you have recourse to fall upon.

Remember that your reputation is on the line as well as the happiness of your bridal couple. The image that the florist sets out reflects on you. The most important thing to remember is that careful planning is essential if you hope to get the most for your client's money, without compromising the beautiful, romantic setting that flowers can add to their wedding day.

One thing that the consultant should be aware of is the meanings of individual flowers. Then when the bride-to-be asks you what flowers you recommend, you will be able to inform her of the meanings of the flowers. This might help her in making her decision if meanings of flowers are important to her.

The Meaning of Flowers

Rose = Love

White Daisy = Purity

Gardenia = Joy

Orchid = Beauty

Carnation = Distinction

Blue Violet = Constancy

Forget-Me-Not = True Love

Red Chrysanthemum = Sharing

Lily of the Valley = Happiness

White Lilac = Youthful Innocence

Photography

Photographers are a very important aspect of the weddings you will be consulting on. Videographers will be discussed separately from photography even though they are related services.   When searching out the best and most professional photographers in your area, you will see that there are a large number to choose from. It is critical that you look in depth at each one and ask questions in detail. You as the consultant must remember that the results of both the photographer and the videographer will be the only visual remembrance of your client's wedding event. They will want the product they receive to accurately and beautifully reflect their wonderful day. Any mistakes in this area will be there forever - no second chances.

The right professional photographer should deliver a complete selection of photographs that tell the full story of the special day. Check out samples of their work, and make sure you ask for customer references. It is important to know how much of the actual work will be done by the photographer and how much will be done by assistants who may have less experience and expertise.

To help select the best professional photographers for your vendor files, use the following questionnaire:

Questions to Ask the Photographer

1. How many photos are usually given in each package?

2. What are the differences in all color, color and black and white and what ratio does the photographer recommend?

3. How many candid photos and how many posed photos will there be?

4. How soon will the proofs be ready after the wedding?

5. Are there extra charges for the proofs?

6. Is there a set number of reprints you must order?

7. What is the cost for additional time or photos?

8. How much is the deposit and when is it due?

9. When is the balance due?

10. Is there a travel charge?

11. Are the negatives available to purchase? If so, do you have to wait a specified time before you can purchase them?

12. What is the photographer's contingency plan in case of illness, family emergency or scheduling conflict.

13. Is it acceptable to use a different source for video than the photography?

14. How many pictures can be expected for the fee that is paid?

Interview as many photographers and review as many wedding albums as you can to find the style that are suitable for your clients. The best photographers tend to be booked months in advance. Inform your clients of the need to reserve your photographer as early as possible.

The costs of professional photography can give the bride and groom sticker shock. As their consultant, you need to understand all the possible photographic possibilities and their cost, so the best decision can be made.

Photographic Opportunities Worksheet

Options	Cost
1. B/W glossy for the newspaper announcement	_____
2. Pre-ceremony portraits	_____
3. Actual ceremony services	_____
4. Formal settings after the ceremony	_____
5. Reception activities	_____
6. Informal groups of family and friends at ceremony	_____
7. Informal group of family and friends at reception	_____
8. Formal bridal portrait (studio)	_____
9. Couple's portrait (studio)	_____
10. Rehearsal dinner shots	_____

Given a small photography budget, numbers 1, 3, 4 and 5 on the list above, would traditionally be considered the minimum photographic coverage.

One last issue must be discussed with the photographer, how the pictures will be bound. Pictures can be bound in four ways. Each has its advantages, and each also comes with a price tag. You need to understand the terminology and be able to explain to the bride and groom the differences in photographic binding.

Four Photographic Bindings

1. Library binding is considered the top of the line and offers the best display of the wedding pictures. This type of binding actually looks like a real book. Photos are individually matted. Then re-matted and then bound in a cover which is often made of leather.

2. Z-Page is the next level of quality and cost. The cover may be simulated leather or a hard cover backing similar to most textbooks. With Z-Page, photos are inserted into a matted page and clamped into place.

3. Post-Bound is similar to Z-Page but the matting process is slightly less expensive and the binding is more susceptible to falling apart over time.

4. Hinge-bound is the least expensive and the least durable. Photos are inserted into paper matting.

One final concern that should be mentioned about the selection of a photographer is personality. The photographer is going to be in and out of almost every aspect of the wedding. You need to consider whether the photographer has a personality that is non-offensive. During the interview process notice how they relate to people. They will be at their best in the interview, so imagine what that person will be like after a long day of working, and when he is no longer worried about securing your business.

Videography

Videography is coming into play more and more often with weddings. Live action of the wedding event has come to mean that the couple can re-play their special occasion over and over and can even make copies for friends and family who were unable to witness the event in person. It is important to make sure that you have thoroughly researched the videographers in your area to be sure that the quality is first rate. As with the photography, this event can only be filmed once. After that, it is just too late.

When interviewing a videographer, ask to see samples of his work. Examine the approach and style of the videographer as well as the sound quality and picture clarity. Of utmost importance is the quality of the editing. Keep these thoughts in mind: What video formats are offered? The formats in order of preference (lowest quality to highest) are VHS, 8mm, Hi8, and SVHS. You should insist that the video be shot at the highest available speed. Does the videographer provide lighting or rely on available light? What are the charges for extra tape? Will the videographer have available back-up equipment in the event difficulties are encountered? Can a photographic/videographic collage be provided? Is a choice of background music, where appropriate, available? Are title screens provided? How many cameras will be covering the events? Has the videographer had experience in conducting on-camera interviews?

Once you have satisfied yourself with the answers to these questions, you will have a professional listing to recommend to your bridal couple.

Limousine Service

Transportation by limousine service is generally the preferred method for getting the bridal party to and from weddings and receptions. Locating this particular vendor is not difficult since there are usually not many limousine services in the average size town. Whatever the number, make sure that you check them out thoroughly. Be certain that the company is licensed and insured. Interview the drivers and see the vehicles yourself to make sure they will be clean. In the contract, specify who will be picked up, when and where. Since pickup times are of extreme importance, you may want to check some of their references to see if the driver was on time as scheduled.

Hotels, Halls and Reception Sites

Accommodating out-of-town guests is no small part of your role as a wedding consultant. This is where you need to locate convenient hotels and motels near the vicinity of the bride and groom. Try to reserve rooms on the same floor, if possible.

Your local Convention and Visitors Bureau can help you locate hotels that are suitable for the couple's guests and will fit within their budget. Ask the hotel you choose to provide you with reservation cards to insert in the invitations. Guests can check off the type of room they need, their arrival time, and method of payment. When you set up the block of rooms, ask the hotel to provide you with a hospitality suite where all the guests of that hotel can meet to visit. If you block enough rooms, this may be included at no cost.

MoneyMaker Tip: When you are able to negotiate special arrangements, like a fee hospitality suite, you have two options. First is to pass the savings on to the customer. The second is to accept those savings as a portion of your fee. Either is considered ethical and acceptable, but everything should be above board when dealing with your customer.

As with any vendor, always obtain a written agreement from the hotel or motel up front. The agreement with the hotel should specify the check-in time, the checkout time, luggage storage, transportation to and from the airport, bus or train stations, reservations, and release or cutoff dates. Be sure to include what the costs would be if the guaranteed rooms are not used or if additional rooms are needed after the cutoff date. You might consider renting an entire Bed-and-Breakfast, since the entire house can be rented for the guests. Check this out with your bridal couple. They could even hold their rehearsal dinner there as a matter of convenience and cost savings.

Provide maps of the city with areas of interest clearly marked for out-of-town guests. This is a courtesy from which guests will benefit and the bridal couple will appreciate. Also, you should provide telephone numbers of taxi services, car rental agencies, bus transportation schedules, and trains and airlines that serve the area.

During the reception, hotel staff are often quite persistent about getting signatures for services they are supplying. As a result, they may approach the mother of the bride or some other person in the wedding party, and can be quite insistent. Make sure from the outset that only one person, you, signs all agreements and no one else is to be bothered.

Remember, the more work you do to please your clients and their guests, the more you will be recommended to others for your efforts. Wedding consultants either lose or gain in the business world by the effort they put into their business. Make yours a success and enjoy the rewards of a job well done!

Checking Out Facilities

When you begin investigating areas for weddings or parties, make sure that they are available for the date your client has chosen. Some dates at country clubs may be booked as much as two or three years in advance. Some hotels prefer not to book events more than three months ahead. And, some popular restaurants are able to prepare an event with only a couple weeks' notice. The number of people on your guest list will help determine what locations to select and how much it will cost. Most important, you must find a location that will accommodate all the guests comfortably.

To gain the trust of your vendors, make sure you enter into your first discussion with them with clear ideas as to what you are expecting from them. Aside from the clarity that they require, you will also gain their respect by showing that you fully understand your (and their) business.

As you look around for appropriate locations for the event you are planning, collect all the information you can about each facility. Most locations prepare information packets they will give you. These packets should contain sample menus and food prices, catering policies, room rates (if applicable), and a room layout guide with seating capacity listed for each room.

Find out what kinds of clientele the businesses you are investigating cater to for the most part. See if they are family, social business or convention oriented. If a hotel is used primarily as a social gathering place, your client may prefer it to one that caters more to conventions.

If you choose a hotel, that hotel is legally bound to hold that space for you once you and they have signed the contract. Generally hotels book their banquet room as much as a year and a half in advance, but most do not confirm dates until three months prior to the clients' planned wedding or party dates.

Wherever you decide to book your event, it is imperative that you check out the grounds carefully. Elderly persons and those with disabilities will need particular consideration. You must be certain that the bride's and groom's guests have access to ramps and ground-level doorways on the outside of the building as well as having elevators inside.

If the bridal couple are planning a live band or a DJ, you need to check the electrical facilities of the reception hall. The band's equipment may place demands on the hotel's electrical system that it won't accommodate.

Make sure that the location you choose has the room for enough tables to accommodate all the expected guests. Round tables allow for a more conversational atmosphere, but they seat fewer people than eight-person, rectangular tables. The bride and groom may have preference about this. If you will require a head table, make sure that you allow space for it. And, if dancing is planned at the reception, you must choose a location that can both seat the guests for the dinner and can also allow adequate dancing area.

Room rates vary according to the season and the popularity of the dates you have requested. September, October, May and June are the most popular wedding months. It is much harder to book exclusive locations during these months. On the plus side, it's easier to negotiate prices and locations in the off months. Be sure to discuss this issue with your clients. November, December and January are the slowest months in most locales. The time between Christmas and New Year's Day in most cities is considered the "dead" period and is the easiest to negotiate.

Deposits are often necessary for most facilities. Often these deposits are non-refundable. Be sure you understand their cancellation policies.

Some services in certain locations are free or included in the overall price. You do need to check to see if liquor is allowed in the establishments you inspect. Some locations charge an extra fee for corkage to serve the liquor to the guests. The same thing goes for cakes. Some hotels charge an additional fee for serving it whether they provide it or not.

If the wedding and reception are Jewish, you must check to see that the establishment will agree to allow specially prepared foods and the kitchen must be kosher.

Most locations automatically set the fees for tips and gratuities. But, this money does not necessarily all go to the waiters, waitresses and other people working at the banquet. It may also be divided among the people who set up the tables and the catering staff, if you use the location's staff for catering. It may also be used as a damage deposit on the room itself. Here are some of the policies you need to be aware of:

- **The meal guarantee:** Most places want you to make your menu selection at least two weeks before the event. Most hotels expect a guaranteed guest count 24 to 48 hours before the actual date. If fewer guests attend, you will not be charged a lesser rate. Therefore you need to be as sure as possible of how many guests you expect. Most caterers plan on serving about five to ten more people than are expected at the event. Usually about five percent of the people you invite do not arrive. If you want to be more careful about the cost and about the amounts of food prepared, give the caterer a guest figure five percent lower than the number you actually expect. You may also discuss leftovers with the caterer. Sometimes you or the bride may be allowed to take them home.

- **Cancellation Charges:** If the wedding is cancelled less than 30 days before the event, you may be charged for rental of the room whether you use it or not. Either way, you will probably be asked to pay a cancellation penalty. Since the hotel's contract is with you, your business will be obligated for this penalty. You need to make sure the bride and groom understand the cancellation penalty obligation so that your business is paid by them.

- **Bar Tab:** If you have a cash bar, the establishment you rent may waive the bartender's fee if you have a specified dollar amount that you will spend. If your bar bill doesn't run that high, you should expect to pay a fee for the bartender in addition to the bill for the drinks. But if the bridal couple is paying for the bar, you must expect to tip the bartender. Some places also charge a gratuity on wine or kegs of beer.

- **Room Rental Fee:** Most hotels have a banquet room charge, which may be waived if your guest list is larger than a certain minimum number. If your guest list is less than 25, for example, you may be charged for the use of the banquet hall as well as for the number of meals served.

- **Bill Payment:** Most establishments prefer being paid in advance for their services or on the day of the event. If you need to make credit arrangements, you must go over this with the caterer when the contract is initially drawn up.

The more you know, the more you will save on your client's wedding and reception and the more profit you will make. Keep in mind that, if you choose to take advantage of it, many vendors will give you a break on cost if you use them consistently.

Hotel Caterers

Caterers will be the most expensive part of your client's wedding. This has been discussed in earlier chapters. Because this is a major expense, it is crucial that you check out the vendors in the area thoroughly. Your judgment and trust mean everything, and you will have to do a lot of taste testing and evaluation to be sure of what you are recommending for your couple.

When the hotel is handling the catering as well as providing the location for the reception, there are some special considerations.

Make sure it is clear whether the caterers are providing liquor or cake in addition to the meal itself. You also need to be clear about their exact charges on a per person basis for each different type of meal. Determine whether they charge by the glass or by the bottle for alcoholic beverages, and if there are extra charges for valet parking, coat checkers, restroom attendants and clean-up.

You must find out if the caterer is insured and what that insurance covers. This is extremely important in the unlikely occurrence of food poisoning or accidental injury. You must go to the establishment not only to see if their food is of high quality (and you'll learn this by tasting some of their dishes), but also to make sure that the caterers are licensed and have health permits in plain sight.

One other area to check out with caterers is whether they charge for delays or re-schedulings caused by acts of nature. If so, what costs will be incurred? And, as with all other vendors, make sure that the contracts you will draw up are clear, in-depth, and leave nothing to chance.

Here are some additional, specific tips:

- **Appetizers** are expensive because they require special preparation, and you need five to seven different choices to satisfy all your guests. Most caterers price their appetizers by the tray and their hot appetizers by the piece, usually with a minimum number of pieces. If you order appetizers in addition to a meal, many will be wasted. If the appetizers are a part of a meal, allow no more than six servings per person. But, if they are all you serve, allow ten to fifteen pieces per person.

- **Buffet meals** are more expensive than meals served at the table. This is because of the preparation time required and the fact that more food tends to be wasted with a buffet. A much larger variety and at least one-third more food needs to be prepared because buffets are an all-you-can-eat, one-stop, serve yourself dinner. At least two entrees, a variety of salads, hot vegetables, and several desserts are offered to the guests.

- **Deserts** may be included in the meals if you are serving a sit-down dinner, but make sure before you sign the agreement.

- **Sample the foods** that are to be served at the event you are planning. Make arrangements with the caterers well in advance so that you can make any necessary changes to the menu in a timely manner.

- **Champagne** - If your clients insist on champagne at the reception, you should inform them that using a champagne fountain is not cost effective. Also, let them know that the champagne in fountains is not kept at a consistently cool temperature and that the bubbles do not last.

- **Ice carvings or sculptures** are an alternative to champagne fountains. They are elegant and can usually be purchased from a student of a chef school for a small fee. The carving can be whatever you desire.

- **Alcohol** is a major moneymaker for hotels and restaurants. There are several ways to charge for alcohol. These include: charge by the bottle, where the full bottle is pro-rated to the nearest tenth, the contents measured, and you are charged for whatever has been used; charge by the drink, where the bartender hits buttons on the cash register that correspond to the drink served; and, charge by the shot, where, if you are ordering a mixed drink, you are paying double for it and even more if you ask for it "on the rocks." Most locations that you seek out for possible reception sites will not allow a caterer or family members to bring in their own alcohol. They can't control alcohol consumption and run the risk of being held liable if someone gets intoxicated and has an auto accident after they leave.

- **Licensed vendors** are the only ones you should contract with. This guarantees that the local health department has approved the caterer and his establishment. Nonetheless, if the food is to be prepared at the caterers' location, inspect his premises yourself for cleanliness. Refrigeration should be adequate, and there must be separate areas for handling raw and cooked foods.

- **Cold foods** should be kept below 40 degrees Fahrenheit for safety and freshness, and hot foods should be kept at least 140 degrees. At the gathering, cold foods can be kept cold by placing dishes on a bed of ice. Chafing dishes keep the hot foods at the proper temperature.

- **Leftovers** can be substantial. Be sure to discuss with the caterer before you sign the contract what is done with leftovers. If you are allowed to keep them, divide them into small portions for quick freezing, but if they are to be refrigerated, use them within one to two days.

There are many things to remember to check for when trying to find your ideal vendors. All the questions are important to the success of your business. Do not be intimidated by any of them. Remember that it is your business, your success, and your livelihood on the line.

Entertainment

Hunting down the best entertainers to recommend to your clients is one of the most exhausting aspects of your job, but it can be one of the most fun. Most of your inquiries allow you to visit the bands on location and hear them in person, which is another legitimate tax deduction. You can deduct going to parties and clubs to hear a bands play!

It's important that you select your entertainment choices carefully. The   music sets the tone for the wedding. Two sets of performers may be required, one for the ceremony and another for the reception. You may, for example, choose a live band, disk jockey, solo singer, piano/organ, harpist or combination of two or more. Wedding bands usually have audition nights at which you can hear them in person. If not, request an audio or videotape. Bridal shows often showcase bands. A wedding consultant with a well-stocked video and audio catalog can be very valuable to the bride and groom.

Many young clients want the latest music played by favorite local bands. That's where the fun comes in for you. It's a good idea to visit local coffeehouses or stage shows to see what you think of the bands in the area. Your musician's personality can add much to the marriage ceremony and can make or break your reception. Once again, don't forget ethnic music preferences.

If your client chooses to use a disk jockey, you must be sure that the ones you recommend are professional and proper. Karoake is becoming popular at receptions, too. Your DJ listing should include some who put on this kind of show. Make sure you know what kinds of music your DJs use and if they are willing to provide whatever types of music the wedding couple prefers.

Questions to Ask Musicians and Disk Jockeys

1. How many breaks will the band take and when?

2. What are the charges for travel time?

3. How much will it be for continuous music and music during the cocktail hour before the reception, if there is one?

As always, obtain a full contract with every musician's name on it and an attached list of the songs you prefer to have played. This contract should include answers to the questions listed above. If you do your homework well, when your bridal couple tells you what kind of music they want at the reception, you will have a foolproof list to offer them.

Music for the wedding and the reception, as well as the musicians themselves, can try your strength when attempting to choose your most valued and professional artists and most requested music. Musical artists, whether a band or a Disk Jockey, are at times difficult to deal with. They have been performing their duties usually for quite some time and can be fairly set in their ways. As with other people who can be difficult, it is helpful to use diplomacy when communicating with them in order to get the bridal couples' needs met.

For instance, a disk jockey might insist on running the whole show his way because that is how most of his clients want it. But, what if your client doesn't? What if your client wants this DJ but prefers a different kind of music or an alternative atmosphere? It is your job to satisfy your client, and it is your strength as a devoted businessperson that will gain that satisfaction. Make sure the DJ understands the expectations; if you have any doubt, either get it in writing or encourage the couple to select another DJ.

Music provides a rhythm for dancing and fills quiet spots in conversations. The chosen music will serve as a mood setter during dinner, and will keep the party or reception going after dinner. Poorly chosen and poorly performed music will end the party faster than any other aspect.

Your clients' musical choice can range from a harp soloist with soft, lilting melodies to a hot-and-heavy rock group. It's totally up to what the bride and groom desire. It's your place to find the right ones to offer as a choice for the couple.

One important consideration is whether the couple prefers a live band or recorded music. If the couple prefers recorded music, make sure you understand what they want. Then make sure the DJ has a large, appropriate library of music to satisfy what they want.

To find what is available in your area, make a thorough search of the Yellow Pages first. You will want to look for booking agents under the listing "Musicians." Almost all bands use an agent. Very few professional musicians advertise on their own due to the fact that it is expensive to take out a Yellow Pages ad, for one thing, and using an agent at a booking agency makes the band or DJ appear more professional. Most agencies will not accept a group or individual if they are not sure of their drawing ability.

Also, an agent will help you find just the right person or group to fulfill your client's needs. An agency will also allow you to preview as many musicians as you wish without making you run all over town. Usually, the agent will also have videotapes of the band or DJ for you to view as well as listen to.

Check out just how long the agent or agency has been in business before you decide to use any particular one. Ask for references. When you are sure of who you will work with on an on-going basis, tell the agent the theme of the occasion and let him or her recommend a group or individual that matches that theme. You must inform the agent as to whether or not there will be dancing and whether you want a variety of musical styles played. You don't want the guests to become bored with only one type.

Whatever you do, do not choose a band or DJ on the basis of the fact that they are the least expensive. You generally get what you pay for in this area. Look and listen for yourself. Choose only on the basis of quality, not price. A good disk jockey will cost about as much as a worthwhile band. If you go with a DJ, make sure that the DJ can entertain guests with more than just musical selections. Stage lighting is important in a DJ-based show. The DJ should also know how to excite the crowd and draw them into the act. They also need to know how to cool the crowd down if the guests become overly involved. And the equipment the DJ uses should be of the highest caliber.

Agencies generally have several DJs on their list, so you must try to see their shows if possible and "name-book" the ones you like best. If you don't do this, you run the risk of having the agency send whomever is available the night of the wedding or reception.

Another consideration with bands as well as DJs is that during breaks, you want your music to continue. You need to discuss with the DJ or band in advance what will happen during those breaks. For example, you must decide if you want the same kind of music that has been playing or if you prefer something softer, allowing the guests to converse more easily as they rest, too.

As with any vendor, get a signed contract! When you hire performers, get everything in writing. Specify the number of musicians. If you are using a DJ, name him! Specify the date and time of the performance and the site of the event. Be sure the contract covers the mode of dress the band or the DJ is to wear.   Also, specify in the contract the number of hours they are to perform and what the charge is if they are asked to stay longer.

Another important point to state in the contract is that you, the consultant (acting for the wedding couple) have the right to determine the volume at which the music is played. And, don't forget to make sure that the site the couple has chosen for the event is equipped with the proper electrical wattage to handle the band's or DJ's equipment.

Within the contract, specify the terms of payment. Find out if you will be paying the agent or the band (or DJ) themselves. Make sure that all charges are clearly stated in the contract. Leave nothing to chance. If needed, separate individual charges and itemize them. Be sure of every detail.

On the following page, you will find an example of a musician's contract. This type of agreement helps ensure you get the services you agreed to, it protects your reputation and ensures the satisfaction of your client.

NOTES

_____

_____

_____

_____

_____

_____

SAMPLE CONTRACT FOR MUSICAL TALENT:

Contract No. _____   Date Mailed: _____

This agreement is null and void unless signed and returned by: _____

1. Date of Contract: _____

2. Name and Address of Place of Engagement:

_____

_____

   City,   State   Zip

3. Name of Band or Act:

_____

4. Number of Musicians: _____

5. Date(s), Starting and Finishing of Engagement: _____

_____

6. Type of Engagement: _____

7. Total Compensation: _____

8. Purchaser will make payments as follows: _____

_____

Purchaser's Name   Name of Band or Act

_____   _____

        Signature   Signature

_____   _____

         Date   Date

Decorations

When it comes time to gather information on decorations vendors, make it a strict point never to trust the way things look in catalogs. You and your client could be very unhappily surprised. It is easy to make articles look better and brighter in a catalog than they actually are in reality.

As you look around at the different stores or businesses that carry decorations and cater to weddings, make sure that they can meet your needs as far as theme, quantity and quality are concerned. This is another area where you don't want to select "second best." It will clearly show. Go only with the best. The only way you will know what the best is, is to comparison shop.

Look over several vendors. Study their products and their pricing. As with all the other vendors you will be dealing with, make sure that what they say they can and will provide is what you will actually get. Only a contract, in clear and concise wording, will guarantee that you do.

You want to find out if particular vendors carry everything you will need or if you will have to deal with more than one. Most professional decorators will be able to supply all your needs. It may take some looking, but reputable decorations vendors are available.

After you have decided whom you will recommend, you must then check with the site you have chosen and see if there are restrictions or limitations on decorations. Some locations limit the number of decorations. Others have time restrictions on what you can do if they are booked shortly before your event is scheduled. Be sure to ask questions of the location's owners/operators before you make plans with your decorator.

The Final Analysis

There are probably other vendors that you may need to service the weddings of some of your couples. If you do not have listings of a vendor for what your couple desires, do some quick yet effective searching so that they will be satisfied and you will be the perfect wedding consultant.

When you first begin to think about becoming a wedding consultant, you may be a little starry-eyed. Visions of beautiful fantasy weddings skirt across your mind, and you just can't wait to be a part of it. But once you get into the business and start interviewing vendors that you will use to perform your first wedding, those fantasies quickly flutter to the back of your thoughts. Reality hits.

Unless you've coordinated major events throughout your life, you probably don't have a lot of experience dealing with vendors in the manner that you will have to from this point on. Restaurants and caterers will take on a different look to you now. Musicians will no longer be people to listen to and enjoy. Hotel managers will no longer be the sweet talking gentlemen they have been until now.   All these people and more are going to become just business people with whom you will have to exercise strength and conviction.

It's easy to get confused when things don't go the way you think they should. Knowing what to expect can make working with these professionals much easier. You will become a very strong professional yourself as you deal more and more with vendors. Eventually, you will know how to bargain with them, getting the vendors to bend to your will.

Some vendors welcome wedding consultants with less enthusiasm than you might expect.   For most of the vendors, weddings are just an everyday part of daily business. To you, however, this is your livelihood, and you must make weddings as big a part of your everyday thoughts as anything else.

You must remember that, even though you have your clients' wedding all planned out, the vendors you will be dealing with may not be able to visualize those plans. It will be up to you to make your desires clearly known to them so that you get exactly what you want. Also most vendors do business only in certain ways, following the policies of their owners. Therefore, you must be able to negotiate with each of them. But never give up on what you want. With gentle, kind, and understanding treatment, most vendors will assist you to the best of their abilities.

Cost is probably the biggest obstacle you will have to overcome with each vendor. It is important that you enter into each establishment and business dealing with an open mind, but with the strength to disagree if you think their pricing is too outrageous.

NOTES

_____

_____

_____

_____

_____

_____

_____

_____

_____

CHAPTER NINE

ALTERNATIVE WEDDING-BASED HOME BUSINESSES

Home-Based Opportunities

As you have already discovered, wedding consulting covers a wide range of businesses, and each is filled with potential for making money, in some cases a lot of money. The role of the wedding consultant is to provide the best possible resources for each client. There may be some services you are able to provide better than anyone in your community. Many consultants actually find these niche areas more lucrative than being a full-service consultant.

The services described on the pages that follow are in high demand today, but few businesses have developed to this point. As a result, you can either conduct an extensive search for these services, or you can develop them as an extension of your own consulting services. In either case, after reading these pages you'll have a better idea whether to begin seeking out these services and or to consider developing the opportunities yourself.

"New Ideas Weddings" Home Business

"New Ideas Weddings" is a wonderful business to undertake. The main requirement you need above all other is creativity. You must be a creative thinker - one who can come up with unique ideas and then can carry them off. Some of them will be not only unusual but could be, purposefully, funny.

You will serve the same purpose as a wedding consultant, but not in the usual way. You aren't planning elaborate, serious, traditional weddings. Yours will be totally different. No two weddings will be alike. And that's what makes this opportunity fun.

One way to advertising this business is to place your very cleverly designed and edited ad in the engagement section of the local and regional newspapers. Make sure that you place ads in every area that contains ads from traditional wedding consultants. You will be in competition with them, and you want your ad to stand out from the rest.

A number of potential clients are not "church goers," but because weddings traditionally occur in a church setting, they often feel they have few choices but to follow that path. For every person seeking a wedding, but who is not involved with a church, you have a potential client if you develop a business in the "New Ideas Weddings" field. Young couples will probably utilize your business more than older couples, but second and even third marriages are also seeking this same unique, memorable twist on their special day. After all, if the "church thing" did not work the first time, maybe there is a way to do it differently?

When marketing your services to niche groups, you must pay special attention to their unique habits. If you want to appeal to young persons who may be more inclined to do less traditional things, remember to create your ads in a manner that appeals to young people.   Run the ad where young people will see, such as in college papers, and local magazines targeted to young people.

You'll also want to design ads that appeal to the older couple, ads that appeal to their interests. These ads may run in classified sections of local magazines, singles bulletin boards for the targeted age group or special publications that are developed around unique interests like country and western clubs or other special themes.

Your success will depend on how you advertise and what unusual types of weddings you can offer. That is where your creative nature kicks in. You have to be ready to plan whatever your client desires.

Because you are the consultant in this case as well as the creator of the couple's dream wedding, you can charge the same rates as the traditional consultant. Your fees will be based on the budget of the couple. Usually you can charge them 15 percent of their total wedding budget.

"New Idea" Weddings Examples

"Period" Theme Weddings - Costumes and trivia from some specific era such as the 1920s or the '60s make up the mode of dress, ceremony, food, and music. The options are limitless.

"Sports Theme" Weddings - Sports decorations are used and the couple and guests come dressed in sports garb complete with tennis shoes. The ceremony would be held in a gym on the court floor. The kind of sport the couple is involved with would be the theme.

"Local or State Park" Weddings - In this wedding, the actual ceremony takes place very informally in a park. The meal is a barbecue complete with picnic tables, grilled food, paper plates and cups. The entertainment could be games, Frisbee and a jam box for music.

"Historic Period" Weddings - This is a wonderful and beautiful dream-filled kind of wedding. The entire wedding features a specific past era. It can be Renaissance, Medieval or Victorian, complete with costumes and decor.

"Winter Holiday" Weddings - If cold weather is not a problem, this is a lovely wedding to put on. The Winter Holiday wedding includes seasonal accents and decorations, velvet dresses, fur trims, and carol singing.

"Weekend Weddings" - These weddings can include about anything the couple desires. The entire guest list in included in the weekend festivities. These can include a major party the day before the wedding, activities planned for the guests as the wedding party prepares for their ceremony, and more partying and fun the day after the wedding. The activities are suggested by the couple, and your job is to carry them out.

"Surprise Weddings" - This is one of the most fun weddings to put on. The couple tells no one what is going to happen. Guests are simply invited to a major "party" that the couple has planned. Only when they arrive do they realize that they are actually attending a wedding.

Only your imagination can limit the opportunities for "New Idea" weddings. Aside from being a good money-maker, this business is loads of fun. As you develop this business, you might find it more lucrative and enjoyable than the traditional wedding.

The one caution about this business niche, is that it is a smaller market than that for traditional weddings. Therefore it is important to continue to serve the market for traditional weddings as well. Make sure you separate these two businesses in your mind, and you may even want to separate them in your marketing campaigns. Different ads, different stationery, different business cards and possibly different phone numbers may be necessary so people do not think of you as only a novelty wedding consultant.

"Bachelor Bashes" Home Business

Another area waiting for your exploitation is the "bachelor bash." These functions have been a long standing tradition with weddings, but few people know where to run to actually have a bachelor bash that is both memorable and tasteful. That's where you come in as a wedding consultant. This is a fun home business that any person can take on.   Everyone knows of the standard bachelor party and its notorious reputation. But bachelor parties can be fun and 'clean' as well.

The ideas for "Bachelor Bashes" are unlimited, depending on your imagination and that of your prospective clients. Themes for these parties could include the "Madness of Matrimony," a staged play with costumes and a special part for the groom to play. Another possibility is what appears to be a standard bachelor party with "stag" movies that turn out to be movies of his life and the life of his fiancÈe. And of course, in the cake that strippers generally jump out of could be his bride!

There are so many possibilities including sports themes, outdoor themes, computer themes and trivial pursuit themes.

As your home business, you would do the planning from your home, meeting with the person who is going to sponsor the bash. You and they would discuss what they want to do for the bachelor, where they want to do it, and what they want you to provide in the way of props and food. In this particular business, you would probably utilize a rental vendor for equipment and other items.

Advertising for this business is a little different. In the others, usually you are talking about how beautiful your product is and how sensitive, etc. In this business, you are going to advertise that your business is wacky, fun, a night to remember! The good thing about this is that if you use the Yellow Pages under wedding services, yours will definitely stand out! As with the other wedding-based home businesses, you want your ad's graphics and text to tell the story of what your business is. It must reflect the attitude and fun of the business. It must draw the people scanning Yellow Pages out of their serious mindset into thinking about what they could do for a light night for the groom. Calling on local consultants to ask that they advertise your business to their brides is another way to get your business known. Again, you can offer a percentage to the consultants.

The good news about being in the "Bachelor Bash" business is that word of mouth travels very fast. You'll build a reputation very fast.

This type of business lends itself well to a human interest article in the local paper. People like to read about these events and you can almost always find an editor to run a feature of you and your type of business. You can also put your ad, possibly along with an article, on the wedding pages of the local and regional newspapers. This could bring in a lot of business.

The rates you can charge for your services would begin with a $20 per hour consulting fee with the sponsor of the bachelor bash. Then, you would charge up to 48 percent above the cost of the rentals, and additionally $20 per hour for the set-up and the take-down of the actual party. For a good bachelor bash, you can expect to make upwards of $700.

The "Bachelor Bash" business can be a terrifically fun as well as a lucrative home-based business. Make this one your own and enjoy!

Wedding Shower and Pre-Wedding Party Arrangers

Many wedding consultants to not want to take the time to actually do the physical labor that is involved in planning a wedding. Most of the consultants prefer doing the planning, then hiring vendors and others to put on the actual affair. This is where the party planner comes in.

You will be the one, under the direction of the consultant, to actually set up and take down the wedding shower and the pre-wedding parties. The consultant would be the one to "hire" you as a sub-contractor. The good part about this business is that the consultant would send the bride to you, and you and the bride would set up the parties.

As for planning the wedding showers themselves, the consultant would send you to the person or people hosting the showers. You and the hostess (or hostesses) would discuss exactly what is desired, the decorations, the theme, and the refreshments (including cakes), and you would take it from there. The bride and her attendants would not have to worry about a thing.

Another very good part of this business is that you have no significant up-front investments to make yourself. The money the consultant would pay you as a sub-contractor would cover the costs of renting or purchasing anything you would need to carry out the party.

Advertising would be as most of the other wedding-based home businesses are: placing ads in wedding sections of newspapers, the Yellow Pages, and, most importantly, letting wedding consultants and bridal shops know of your business and your skills in throwing amazingly fun pre-wedding parties.

The fee you would charge would be about $15 an hour, including the consultation time with the party-giver. The profit is 100 percent - a wonderful way to earn money and have fun at the same time. A fee of $500 - $700 is certainly possible.

Wedding Stationery Designers

A fourth niche business is the wedding stationery design business. This business is a good sideline for persons who want to work from home. It is a business that can be quite lucrative. If your creative skills are fully developed and you have desktop publishing skills, this is a natural business for you. Of course, this means having access to both a computer and a color printer. If you already have a personal computer at home, you will have very little cost outlay for beginning this exciting business.

Weddings, like most businesses today thrive on printed materials. Here are just a few things your business can provide that every wedding must have: invitations, announcements, thank-you notes, personal stationery, place cards and paper place mats. Your service can also include pick-up and delivery, and if you can provide the service and the appropriate equipment, you can also print these products directly from your home, although this will require a fairly substantial investment to buy the appropriate copiers and printers.

Advertising this service can be a relatively inexpensive venture. One way to advertise is to watch the local newspapers for persons who are newly engaged. You can attempt to contact these persons and contract directly with them. Another easy way to advertise and gain business is to contact each wedding consultant in your area and in other remote areas and explain what you can do for them. Ask them to refer their clients to you. You may also offer the consultant a percentage of your profits if she will use you as one of her continually used vendors.

Direct mail is another way to advertise your business. You can mail samples of your work along with a letter of introduction to all the printers in your area. You could promise to use their services if they recommend you as a designer.

The rates you could charge for your initial design services vary, but the average initial design rate runs about $50-$100, depending upon the extent of the design. Then you can charge for printing, if you choose to perform this service as well. The amount of the charge depends upon the quantities and quality of paper products the couple chooses to use. If you charge by the hour, a typical rate is $20 per hour.

One of the best advantages of this service for the bridal couple is that you are offering uniqueness, something that will never be duplicated by other couples. You will create a unique, one-of-a-kind design that reflects the wants and needs of this one particular couple. No other couple will have the same thing.

Wedding Writers

The job of wedding writer is two-fold. One segment includes addressing, stamping envelopes, filling out and stuffing invitations and announcements using calligraphy or other approved script. The second segment is the writing of wedding vows.

The first segment, that of taking care of the invitations for the bridal couple, is one that is extremely time consuming for the bride and her groom. It is a huge load off her mind if she can find someone to take over this enormous task for her.

The way to begin this business is to acquire the skills of accurate and professional calligraphy. Many art stores offer classes in calligraphy. Calligraphy is a beautiful script that is the most commonly used script in wedding announcements and invitations. Once you turn this skill into a craft that you know is better than anyone else's in the area, you are on your way.

The costs of starting up this business are quite minimal in that the only tools required are a professional set of calligraphy pens, nibs, and inks. Of course, for formal invitations and announcements, black ink would be the accepted color.

The cost of professional quality calligraphy sets runs from $16.25 to $25.99, depending on the brand that you choose. Additional ink cartridges average $4.60 for a set of six. Not a bad investment for what you as a professional calligrapher can earn.

After gaining the skill of a professional calligrapher and purchasing the equipment, you only need to determine a location in your home that will be out of the way of anyone or anything that might possibly cause a mess of your work. You will need a table that will allow you to spread out your materials, leaving you plenty of room to stack the announcements and invitations and for you to work. It's necessary to keep blotter tissues on hand, as well.

Another segment of the "wedding writer" business involves the actual writing of wedding vows for the bride and groom. Sound silly? It's not. All couples who marry have thoughts of romance and commitment that they feel about each other, but many people don't know how to express these thoughts. That's where you come in.

Your skills as a writer can be the one to develop these terms of endearment for the bride or groom. You are the one to put their feelings into words that they can either read or memorize to recite to each other on their perfect day. There is absolutely no expense to start up this business other than the costs of advertising, which, as with the calligraphy, can be minimal.

One of the best ways to advertise these businesses is to follow the engagement announcements in the newspapers. Contacting these couples and discussing your unique business with them can bring in plenty of business for you. Then adding in the additional skills of calligrapher and the service you can offer them in this regard, should solidify your business relationship.

Another method of advertising is the Yellow Pages of your telephone directory. Make sure that it is listed in the wedding services section. A beautiful ad, designed by you in your best calligraphic style, will catch the eye of brides and grooms who are searching those pages for other wedding businesses.

The rates that you can easily charge for your services are a minimum of $20 per hour. With the time you would save the bride and groom for their announcements and invitation addressing alone would make these rates well worth it to them. And the beautiful sentiments you would write for the bride and groom for their wedding vows could never be discounted. The couple would be so enthralled with how you put their feelings into words that the cost would not be considered.

In both these areas, your skills and the way you please the couple would be an automatic advertisement. Just be sure that your professionalism clearly shows through.

The Wedding Decorations Home Business

This is a wedding business that can earn you a lot of money if you market yourself correctly and are incredibly creative and artistic. Fortunately, for most wedding entrepreneurs, weddings are a very emotional, sentimental time. Those who are in charge of making the plans are smitten by things that are lovely and hit the emotional chord. This is your chance to be a part of a wonderfully beautiful business.

The wedding decorations business is perfect for your home because you can have the room in your basement or a spare bedroom where you make-up the decorations. And neither creativity nor design limits what you do. Whatever you create in your head or on paper or from playing with your materials, if you handle it right, it can sell!

Start-up costs for this business are varied. If you choose to show your wares at bridal shows or even flea markets, the cost isn't substantial. You pay only the cost of the table you rent and getting your products to the set-up area. For this type of business, however, we strongly urge you to create a professionally designed catalog for showing what you can do. If you are computer literate or have a friend who is, then this can also be done at home.

Design your own logo, after deciding on a name for your company. Make sure the name and the logo reflect clearly what your business is. Be clever and creative with this. If you can find someone with a color printer that prints legal sized paper, you can print your own catalog on slick paper at a minimal cost. Until you are sure that your products will sell, and until you find vendors who will assist you with your advertising (placing your catalogs or recommending you for your product), you don't want to go to the expense of hiring a professional printer. Start small and build fast.

The major cost for you in the beginning is gathering materials for your designs. And of course, you must decide what you want to make first. If your products use lots of dried or silk flowers, for instance, then you could talk with a flower vendor and offer a swap. You could ask the vendor to sell your products or recommend you for special wedding items if you would agree to purchase all your flower supplies from him. Or you may be able to sell your wares in the florist shop on consignment. That works quite often.

Circulate your catalogs among local consultants as well. Ask them to use you as a vendor for decorations in exchange for offering her a slight percentage of your sales to the couple.

You can also visit bridal clothing shops and ask them the same. Leave your catalogs everywhere that might pertain to weddings. Make sure that your catalogs have color photos of your designs and products and that they have clear, understandable descriptions and prices (if the prices will remain the same for a while).

While waiting for customers, work at home building up a selection of everything that is in your catalog. And, by the way, in this catalog and in all your advertising, make sure that you let your prospective customers know that you can and will make decorations to their own design, if possible. This makes your business unique and special. Not all decoration vendors will do this.

Advertise in the wedding sections of the newspapers, too. And don't forget about placing an ad in the Yellow Pages in the weddings section. Most importantly, word of mouth is going to get you further than any "paid for" advertising. Make your products special, make a bride happy, and your business will grow.

"New Home Set-Up" Home-Based Business

Here is a business that can be loads of fun, as well as one major load of work! This business of setting up households for a newly married couple allows you to kind of live out some of your dreams. It's a great business for couples, too. Since there can be some heavy lifting, sharing the chores with your mate can be a very good idea.

New Home Set-Up is a good business because it takes zero capital other than having a truck to haul items to the new home, if necessary. Sometimes, the bride and groom or one of their family members will have the items sent there for you.

What this job would involve would be simple. All you need to do is take all the gifts that the couple received and put them in order in the new house or apartment. Included in the business is cleaning the new living quarters, changing linens, setting up the bathrooms, etc. Anything that you can do to prepare the house or apartment for the newlyweds to come home to is what this business is all about.

As far as expenses go, you would provide the cleaning products you would use in getting the quarters in order. You need to carry insurance against breakage, injury and theft. You need this protection in the event something goes wrong while you are on their premises.

With this business, you can easily charge $20 per hour for your efforts. For this pay, you would make sure that when the new couple enter that house or apartment, they will see shining mirrors, totally clean carpets and floors, a freshly made bed, and an immaculate kitchen.

Advertising is as in the other businesses. But this business is unique, making it an easy one to start. There is very little competition. The way you advertise and the service you provide must be unique as well. Find ways to distinguish your services from those offered by others in this business. For example, one nice way to do this is to leave an attractive basket of fruit and flowers on the dinner table, with a lovely card from your service. If you can do it, also include a bucket with a nice bottle of champagne and two special personalized glasses for the couple.

The more you do to please them with your work and show them how much care you've taken, the better you look. This alone will gain more business for you. And for your work, you get the satisfaction of knowing that you did all you could to make a real impression on the new lives of two special people.

A Final View-Point on Creating a Home-Based Business

One of the major hurdles that must be overcome when starting any home-based business is generating initial business. Each of the ideas suggested in this chapter are immediate sources of revenue, and each could actually become a full-time business on its own, until your consulting business is underway. If you examined the reasons for success and failure of home-based businesses, you would see that one of the biggest is dealing with the need for immediate cash flow. One of the real advantages to the wedding consulting business is that it provides a wide variety of quick revenue streams. This is one of those businesses where you just jump in and see what works.

NOTES

_____

_____

_____

_____

_____

_____

_____

_____

CHAPTER TEN

QUESTIONS AND ANSWERS FOR THE WEDDING CONSULTANT

Overview

As you begin your business, numerous questions will arise. In the previous chapters we have addressed the major issues that surround the business of wedding consulting, but there are still many questions that do not fit neatly into those chapters. We attempted to answer those questions in this final chapter.

Q: I am having problems with vendors who have become my friends. It is so hard to keep things on a business level. Do you have any suggestions?

A: This is a common problem. As your business grows, you will become good friends with some of your best vendors, and the line between business and friendship will blur. The best recommendation is to make sure the customer evaluates every service your provide and that you de-brief the service with each service provider. By using a Wedding Day Satisfaction Rating Worksheet, you can discuss business issues without getting friendship tangled up in the discussion. You will simply be talking about how a customer evaluated the service. This will keep the discussion on a business and professional level and avoid getting things on a personal level.

Q: How do you recommended I handle a situation where I have not been contracted   for a particular service at the wedding, but on the day of the wedding something goes wrong and there is no one around to help?

A: This is probably going to happen on a regular basis if you stay in the business of wedding consulting. You will have a relationship with most of the vendors, and if you are good they will turn to you for help without thinking about it. They may not even be aware that you are not contracted for the service at that moment.

The fundamental point in this question is for you to decide what your purpose is for the wedding. If it is to make the day as perfect and hassle free as possible, then you will do what it takes to make that happen regardless of the contractual relationship you have with the bride and groom.

Should you inform the family of what you did? Probably not at that time, but you will certainly have an opportunity to mention it when you provide your post-wedding appraisal. Here are two forms on the following page to help you with post wedding evaluation.

Wedding Day Satisfaction Rating Worksheet

How did your wedding go? Please tell me whether we made your wedding perfect in every way we could. On a scale of 1 to 4 please rate the following services. If we did not provide consulting in an area, please circle N/A.

	Low		High		

General Rating

1. Rate the overall service you received ? 1 2 3 4 N/A

2. How well did we keep you informed? 1 2 3 4 N/A

3. How did we do at making everything hassle free? 1 2 3 4 N/A

4. Did we do everything we promised we would do? 1 2 3 4 N/A

Pre-wedding Services

5. Rate the quality of information and help you received? 1 2 3 4 N/A

6. Were we able to answer all your questions? 1 2 3 4 N/A

7. Rate our availability while planning your wedding. 1 2 3 4 N/A

8. Did we handle bachelor and bridal parties as expected? 1 2 3 4 N/A

Wedding Ceremony

9. Rate the quality of the decorations. 1 2 3 4 N/A

10. Did we do what you expected during the service? 1 2 3 4 N/A

Reception Services

11. Rate our reception services 1 2 3 4 N/A

12. Did we handle problems and questions so you were free to

be with family and friends during the reception? 1 2 3 4 N/A

13. What did we do best?

14. What needs improvement?

15. Would you unconditionally recommend us to your friends?

   Yes [   ]   No [   ]

16. May we use your name and ratings in our marketing and advertising?

   Yes [   ]   No [   ]

Post Wedding Evaluation of Services

The following evaluation of your services is provided to help you maintain the quality of your services and to ensure that we can continuously improve our business. Please review this evaluation, and then rate my work with you on the bottom half of the form and return it to me. Thanks for you help.

Low   High

My Rating of Your Services

1. Overall quality of your product/service   1 2 3 4

2. Timeliness of services   1 2 3 4

3. Overall appearance of your product/services   1 2 3 4

4. Knowledge and expertise of your product/service 1 2 3 4

5. Ability to resolve problems   1 2 3 4

6. Kept me informed of changes   1 2 3 4

Please help me improve my services by completing this rating.

1. Please rate the overall quality of my services   1 2 3 4

2. Did I keep you informed in a timely manner   1 2 3 4

3. How well did I use your services   1 2 3 4

4. Was I helpful if any problems came up?   1 2 3 4

5. Do you have advice for me?

Return to: [*Insert your name here*]

                    [*Insert address*][*Phone*]

Q. It seems as if there are as many churches in this community as there are
people. How does a wedding consultant learn about all the religious
traditions and ceremonies clients might ask for?

A. Fear of being caught off guard lies underneath this question. If you are asked
to consult on a wedding that is highly religious and unfamiliar to you, you are
more than likely going to have a fair amount of help from the clergy. Make a friend of
the clergy and you will receive a lot of support from them. Be very clear and direct
with the clergy stating your goal for the wedding and then ask for help. The following
questions will usually obtain more than enough information to keep you from being
embarrassed.

"What special arrangements are necessary to meet your customs and practices?"

1. "Are there any special features of a wedding in your faith that are unique and
   that I should be aware of?"

2. "If there is an area where the bride or groom could be embarrassed, what would
   it be?"

3. "Since I will be making the arrangements for the entire wedding, from
   photography to reception, are there customs people from out of town will
   expect, that I might not be familiar with?"

4. "Are there any unique dietary or clothing practices we should accommodate
   during this wedding?"

5. Are photographs allowed during the ceremony?

Wedding consultants generally have a problem with church practices when their
client is marginally practicing their faith. During your get-acquainted meetings, ask
the couple what they believe are the customs they should follow, and assure them
that you will talk to their clergy to make sure what must be done. When you carry
this burden, they do not have to ask their clergy questions they are "supposed" to
know the answer to.

Q. Do you have a recommendation for handling conflict with the client when
problems happen?

A. It is important to remember that conflict is simply a sign that someone's
needs have not been met. In a wedding, that usually means that someone, or
some thing has failed to meet expectations. Written agreements are one of the best
ways to handle these expectation gaps. Simply turn to the promises in question and
show on paper what was agreed to. THEN, ask the client what they would like in

addition to what was promised. The goal is not to prove them wrong, but to make sure you and the client are going in the same direction.

Q: When meeting with other wedding consultants and different vendors, how confidential should I be about my fees?

A: This is a matter of personal preference for most consultants. We advise being open and honest about your fees. After all, you are going to talk to clients about those fees, so it will be hard to guard your prices. If, however, you are being under-cut on prices and find that you are losing customers, it is time to adjust your fees and ask clients for confidentiality.

Q: I am not very good at negotiating. Do you have any tips?

A: Negotiating is a learned skill. There are a number of books and seminars that can help you sharpen your abilities. But before you enroll you might want to think about your specific questions about negotiating.

Most people have no experience at negotiating except for occasional dealings with car salesmen. Inexperienced vs. professional negotiators...no contest! No wonder you believe you can't negotiate. It is very hard to deal when you are emotionally wrapped up in the deal. After all, you really want that car!

Most negotiating will result when working with vendors. Although you might find yourself asking for a better commission, usually you are trying to get a better price for your customer. You may care a great deal, but usually you are not caught in the emotional trap you are accustomed to. Most people find negotiating on behalf of someone else fairly easy.

Generally, you will not find yourself negotiating with clients. They either accept your fees or they don't. If you bargain too much on your professional fees, you minimize your value.

Q: I've heard a lot of nightmares about the wedding rehearsal. Do you have any guidelines that can make them a little more fool proof?

A: Here are a some general guidelines every consultant should hold fast and follow.

1. All members of the wedding party must attend the rehearsal. Often due to very busy schedules and out of town travel, couples will attempt to cut corners and just get by. It is easy to assume that the only people who need to practice are the bride and groom, which could not be further from the truth. If you want a beautiful wedding you must rehearse. Your client is spending thousands of dollars for this special day, do not let them short change themselves. If a key person, no matter how special, cannot be in the rehearsal, give them a different role. If the consultant gets very specific commitments early in the planning, and categorically asks people to participate in the rehearsal, this can usually be overcome.

2. Make sure copies of the ceremony program are provided to all participants for the rehearsal. Few people will study the program before the rehearsal, but you should make sure copies are made and handed out at the rehearsal. Do not expect people to share.

3. Follow the instructions of the officiant for the specific details regarding your ceremony. Usually the clergy will have a very specific strategy for getting everyone prepared. Consider yourself an assistant to the clergy. You may want to call or meet early with the clergy and ask what you can do to help.

4. Rehearse with music. Although this may cost extra, weddings are choreographed around music. You cannot possibly practice the wedding without the music. This practice also helps ensure that the musicians are truly prepared.

5. Do not over-rehearse the children in the wedding party. Kids usually get confused with excessive practice. Most of the spontaneity of a wedding ceremony comes from the kids. Don't take it away.

6. Tell all ushers to arrive at least one hour early on the wedding day.

Q: I know you talked about fees and service charges throughout the book, but can you provide some simple ways for me to charge for my services as a consultant?

A: The bottom-line on all fees, is to determine what your knowledge and time are worth. Here are several ways other wedding consultants bill for their services.

1. Some consultants charge an hourly fee. The more time you spend on the wedding, the more the client pays. This is the way many attorneys bill for their services. A wedding consultant's hourly fees range from $35 - $70 per hour.

2. Some consultants have a rate chart for their services, similar to a chart of services a physician might use. The rate chart fees are set based on the magnitude of the services.

3. Many consultants charge between 7% and 15% of the total cost of the wedding.

4. Many consultants are paid a booking fee by the vendors they use. This can range from a flat fee of $25 to as much as 10% of the vendor's fee.

5. If you are providing multiple services, it is advisable to break the fee into its component pieces, so the client knows exactly what they are paying for, and you know exactly what is expected.

Q: Do you have any other recommendations about advertising?

A: The most powerful marketing source is word of mouth. Make sure you ask every client and every vendor for referrals. It is also important to always be thinking promotion. Whenever you deal with friends of the family, and even clergy, remind them of your business.

The home-based business of wedding consultant can be exciting, fun and quite profitable. It can also be extremely rewarding personally because of the joy and peace of mind you can bring to the lives of your clients on what is to them a very special occasion. Perhaps the most rewarding aspect of all, however, is that unlike being employed by someone else, you will get everything out of this business that you put into it. Most of all, when you succeed, you will have the pleasure and satisfaction of knowing that you did this for yourself and your family. Best of luck and success as you get started!

NOTES
